# Candle M[...] & Home-B[...] Start-up

### Guide to Candlemaking, Building a Customer Base, Branding & Marketing

### Proven & tested Tips on Packaging, Pricing, Selling, Social Media Ads & Safety!

**By**

# Ally Russell

Published by:

**Streets of Dream Press**
Cover & Interior designed

By

Jackie Robinson

*First Edition*

# TABLE OF CONTENTS

# CHAPTER 1: AN INTRODUCTION

Congratulations on purchasing this book! With this, you've taken the first – and often, the hardest – step of your journey. You are officially on your way to owning your very own business, doing something that is both creative and fun. Imagine, making money while having fun!

You should be excited. Feel excited! As you read through this book, try to maintain the optimism and anticipation you feel right now. Keep that positive outlook as you buy your supplies, plan your space, and start your journey.

Whatever you do—don't quit. It's going to be scary and sometimes overwhelming. Anything hard is going to feel like that at first, after all. But if you keep your momentum, and your eyes on the end goal, you can absolutely make your dream a reality. Slowing down now, or halfway through, means it will take you longer to get to the finish line: a successful, thriving candle business.

If you picked up this book, more than likely you've made your own candles before. But—whether you've never made a single candle in your life, or you've made dozens and now you're ready to take the next step—I've got you covered.

Let's begin this journey, shall we? You've taken the initiative yourself – buying this book, making the decision to start your own business, getting serious. Now, we'll get started together.

## Introduction: Who Am I?

You might be asking yourself: Who is this person, and what do they even know about candle making? Or business? That's a fair question, and I understand your concern. If we're going to make this journey together, learning about starting and running a successful candle-making business, you might as well know a little bit about me.

I've had my own candle-making business for over 10 years now. My obsession with candle making started relatively innocently, too. I loved candles, but certain brands, scents, and types of candle wax gave me terrible headaches. It was so disappointing, and for a long time I just didn't burn any candles.

One summer, though, I stopped moping around about my lack of candles and decided I wanted to do something about it. I did lots of research, had plenty of trial and error, and finally produced a candle that I really liked. It wasn't as hard as I was expecting once I got the kinks worked out, and the final product smelled great, had a good burn time, and didn't make my head ache. I felt so proud of myself.

That year, I gave handmade candles to all of my friends and family as gifts. I tried to customize their candles to what scents I thought they would like, and it was a big hit. A few months later, I got my first "real order": My best friend asked me to make candles as favors for her wedding.

I soon realized we were talking about 150 guests, custom labels, a custom scent made for her. I was in over my head, completely overwhelmed, and almost missed the deadline. But I made it! Nearly 200 custom candles (the bride and groom kept several for mementos), all ready to be given away for her big day.

At the actual wedding, I was happily surprised that many people loved my product. I had at least a dozen people come up to me asking if I really made the candles or just put labels on them. Several people asked me for my business card, and a few talked about doing custom scents and candles for their own businesses or events.

Business cards? New orders? Look, I did these in my basement basically the week before the wedding—I didn't have a storefront. I didn't have a website. But I realized—when the third person was talking to me about it—that instead of doing the

Cha-Cha Slide, I needed all of these things and more.

I took down names and numbers. I gave out my number on the back of napkins and apologized, telling people that I had "completely forgotten" my business cards at home, but I would get with them.

Thus, my candle making was upgraded from a personal hobby to a real-life business, a blessing for a busy mom. Not only that, but I also got into making and selling my own soap, as you can see in my other books. And I've never looked back.

Okay, that's a lie – there have been hard days. Hard months, even, when I've struggled and sometimes wished I hadn't made those candles for that wedding. Struggling, though, is a part of growth; and I've pushed through those moments to come out stronger and happier on the other side.

As you may have guessed, I had zero business experience going into this. I had no idea what marketing was or how to do it. I didn't understand social media, building a brand, or even how SEO worked. There is so much to building a candle-making business—which is why I wrote this book to help walk you through it.

I did it alone, so you don't have to. I tried and failed and struggled, so you don't have to.

We'll take this journey together. Learn from my mistakes, and you can find success in your own business. It won't always be easy, but it will be worth it.

## Why Candles?

I've gotten this question a lot over the years. Why candles? Why not perfume or woodworking or knitting or--? There are dozens of hobby-businesses that you could fill in the blank with, and the question would be a valid one.

So let's talk about candles. Obviously, something about them appeals to you. Though most people take them for granted, they can completely change an atmosphere. You'll find them sitting on shelves, in the center of coffee tables, or on a dresser. During a nice dinner, maybe when someone has friends over, they'll light one and remember just how pleasant burning a candle can be.

No wonder people love them. Fun fact: 8 out of 10 households in the US have candles, buy candles, and burn candles. That is a huge market! Nearly everyone loves a good candle.

According to numerous scientists, the sense of smell is the sense that is most closely tied with memory. It only takes a little hint of a familiar scent to bring us back to a time or place in our memories, and this is because of the way the human brain is wired.

Let's get technical, just for a moment. The olfactory bulb is a structure at the very front of your brain, and it handles all of the smells that come in through your nose. The olfactory bulb then sends out commands to the rest of your body, and this happens quickly – such as, this smells really excellent, let's let the stomach know; or this smells dangerous or vile, let's avoid. They also travel straight through the body's limbic system, which includes the amygdala and the hippocampus.

These regions are tied to both emotion and memory.

It's no wonder a scent can evoke such a powerful feeling or emotion: It's literally hardwired into us.

Some might ask, why candles? For me, it's a clear answer – we're hardwired to love scents, and we associate them with specific times and places in our lives. Scent is everything, and a candle is one of the best long-lasting carriers of that scent. Of course, candles. Why would I do anything else?

## More Than a Hobby

If you're only considering making candles as a hobby, that's okay. Maybe you're just going to start doing candles for yourself, or your friends and family, and you just want to see where they take you. That's okay, too. This book can still help you.

There is a ton of information I've gathered here for you, including types of candles, types of wax, the tools you need, how to pour your candles, how to burn your candles—there is so much to know. Even if you're not sure about the 'business' side of things, but you're really interested in the 'candle' side of things—don't worry, there is something in here for you.

Who knows? Maybe you'll start doing candles just for yourself, and it will snowball into a business, just like it happened to me. Or maybe you'll start pouring candles and find that you don't love the mass production and want to keep it a small-scale operation for special occasions or select customers. That's totally okay, too.

I can't stress enough – this is your journey! Do what you need to do to make your dream a reality, whatever your dream looks like. It doesn't have to make you a ton of money to bring you joy.

# CHAPTER 2: MOVING ON UP

To make this resource more valuable to you, I'm going to make an assumption – you've made a candle before. Heck, you've probably made a few candles. You have an idea of the basics, and you're ready to dive in and really start making more. But maybe you're not quite sure how to 'level up' your process to a larger scale.

Perhaps you don't love your own process and wish it were more streamlined. Or you're interested in new methods, new tools, new equipment. Whatever the case, you're here to learn more.

Let's talk a little bit about what you're going to need to upgrade to this new business of yours. I've included the bare minimum of what you'll need, plus how to get it cheaply, below. Feel free to ignore my suggestions and get the most expensive options, or jump into the deep end and just buy everything you can think of.

Remember, however, that you can always upgrade later. If you're not sure you need the most expensive option, it's absolutely okay to go with the cheaper one; and in six months, if your production is more intense, you can upgrade. In fact, I recommend going with this strategy for many things. Why?

Your needs are going to change as you go on. Maybe you start out only making one or two types of candles, but as you expand, you decide to add a few more. Now, you need newer tools. Or let's say you only start as a small side hustle, and six months in, you're getting blown out of the water with orders. Suddenly you need more space, bigger equipment. So if you had spent a ton of money on everything starting out, it would have hurt a lot more financially to replace and upgrade it all.

Smaller start-up costs mean you can put more money back into your business; it's as simple as that.

Ready to learn what you need? Get a pen and paper, and start taking notes!

## Your Workspace

You're going to need a space to make your candles, obviously.

But wait. Don't shell out money renting space right at first. Put down your phone, close your internet browser, and pause for a second. Especially when you're starting out, you don't really need to rent a space. The biggest mistake I see people making when they start a business like ours is they go all out getting the biggest space with the best features, and their overhead becomes unmanageable before they ever pour their first candle.

You do not need to pay for space. At least, not necessarily, and certainly not right away. As you scale up, you might find that you do need to rent more space for production and storage, but you should work your way up to that point. The lower you keep your startup costs now, the more likely you are to be able to continue.

Instead, let's talk a walk around your house. Do you have a basement? A garage with electricity? A spare bedroom? Even an unused dining room? (I'm not judging.) These are all good choices for where your brand-new business can start.

The absolute minimum you're going to need is a safe, clean, dedicated space to work. An area without major distractions is nice, but if you can't swing it right away, make do. You can even put up temporary walls to help close yourself off from the rest of the house.

Electricity is a must for multiple reasons, so choose somewhere that you can have lights at the very least, if not heat and air. If you're starting your candle business in the middle of winter and it's 10 degrees outside each day, a space heater might be needed for an area that is not always warm enough to be comfortable in. If it's the middle of summer and you're not in a cooled area, you'll need plenty of fans and circulation. And you don't want it to be so hot that your candles melt, believe me.

If you don't have enough space, don't be afraid to ask friends or family if they have a space that you could rent for a few months. An extra garage your in-laws aren't using, a big corner of your sister's unfinished basement, or even a neighbor's shed they haven't opened in years.

Once you've got your area squared away, let's talk about what you need inside of your space.

## Furnishing Your Work Area

I mentioned you need electricity – this is because you really, really need light. Having a well-lit area is a must, so get those extra-bright bulbs in any sockets where you don't already have them now.

A portable, easy-to-move light source is ideal for more rustic areas, and you can get work lights relatively inexpensively at most hardware stores. Remember that it doesn't have to look great right now; it just has to function. You're a baby business; no one is expecting your workspace to be on the cover of a magazine.

Personal tip: I really love plant lights that have adjustable light settings and clip onto the side of tables. You can usually pick up a few for pretty cheap, and they tend to be reliable, bright, and have adjustable arms so you can get the light exactly where you need it. For $20 or so, I can light up a workbench like it's daytime—literally!

A workbench is your next investment, and this is a must. It's really tempting when you're shopping online to go for the super-stylish, super-cute workbench that would make you feel sleek and professional. But honestly? I encourage you to stay away from those entirely.

Instead, look for a sturdy, well-built workbench that can withstand lots of use, heat, and abuse. You're going to be using this for several hours a day, hopefully for years to come, so you need to make sure it lasts. Workbenches that are made for woodwork or other heavy industries are going to be your best choice.

If you're concerned about money, you can probably make your own workbench, but you can also look on Craigslist, Facebook Marketplace, or other second-hand selling sites to see if a business or individual is looking to offload their older workbench for cheap. You can upgrade to the bench of your dreams once you're set and successful. But to start with, put the money where it matters—back into your business.

Staying organized is going to be your biggest hurdle. Okay, perhaps I'm projecting, and staying organized was my biggest hurdle. But keeping everything where it belongs is so important. There is less struggling and hunting for what you need, and more actual time spent making your product.

Shelves are a big deal, and I encourage you to label them as well. Everything you use should have a 'home' or a place it belongs. When you're done for the night, you should return everything to its 'home' on your shelves. Tools, supplies, and more – they all should belong somewhere. If you stop clutter right away, your workspace will always be clean and organized.

Personal tip: Check out restaurant supply stores for big wire shelving units. They're going to be a lot cheaper than more 'traditional' shelving choices, super sturdy, and hold a lot of weight. No, they aren't the most attractive choice you can make, but they will last you a long time and hold up to any abuse you have to throw at them.

Make sure you also have a place to store finished products as well. And think long and hard about where you're going to store them. If you live in a hot climate, you can't exactly store your candles in the garage or out in the sun. They will melt before they ever get to your customers!

It doesn't need to be refrigerated, of course, but a climate-controlled space for your goods is important. A basement or a spare room are both perfect.

How to store your products while you're waiting to send them to their new homes is another consideration. I like using stackable bins, and I just put white masking tape on the bin. Then, with a black marker, I write exactly what is inside that bin. That way I don't have to go searching around when

I'm trying to find something. I can rip the tape off and replace the label without a lot of hassle.

## What Tools Do You Need?

You're ready to furnish your workspace, and now it's time to think about the tools of the trade you're going to need to be successful. Some of these are obvious; some aren't – but you'll need them all if you want your production to happen.

**Wax melter**: You're going to need some way to melt and mix wax, and I recommend either a double boiler or a rice cooker to start with. You can create a double boiler by using a wide pot to heat the water, and a metal pitcher with a handle (for the wax) that sits taller inside the first pot. It's a good idea to look up some online videos if you've never used a double boiler before. There are several candle-making pitchers or pouring pots available online, many of which are relatively inexpensive. A gentle, low heat is ideal for any type of wax (we'll talk about types of wax next, so stay tuned). You absolutely can purchase an industrial-grade wax melter for larger scale production, but know these will usually cost you over $1,000. For your first startup, sticking with the cheaper option is probably better.

**Jugs** or **pots** to pour and mix your wax are essential, and I recommend using plastic ones. Why? These are lighter, so they are a lot easier to lift and use repeatedly over long periods of time; they are a lot cheaper; and if you drop one of these, well, it will bounce – or at least thud. You will not get pieces of your jug everywhere or have to throw out a lot of what you've done because it could be contaminated.

**Pipettes** are narrow tubes for measuring liquids. You're going to feel like you're running a science project when you purchase these, but they are so easy to use and easy to clean. Plus, in my experience, you get a more accurate final product.

A **thermometer** is key to getting a good reading on your wax and having an accurate and repeatable final product. I would go so far as to recommend starting out with an infrared thermometer, even if it's a little more expensive than the traditional one.

Infrared thermometers do not have to be immersed in the wax to gauge the temperature. Using a traditional thermometer will leave it sticky and covered in wax and could result in an inaccurate read. An infrared thermometer, however, will show you an accurate read, and it won't be a hassle to clean.

Disposable **gloves** are going to be your best friend for keeping wax, scents, and coloring off of your skin. When I started, I would just get food-grade gloves from the local restaurant supply store, but you can buy them almost anywhere now.

**Fire safety** is no joke, so don't treat it like one! A handful of fire blankets should be within easy reach at all times. In addition, I highly recommend at least one fire extinguisher in your space that is regularly inspected and maintained. This is truly an expense you cannot cut.

You're going to need **electricity** in all of your space, so extension cords and a large surge protector that will let you plug in multiple devices at once are going to be a must! Check your local computer supply shop for the best deals.

**Stirring spoons** are essential because you're going to be stirring a lot. You're going to want something easy to clean and easy to store. Wooden spoons just aren't going to cut it – the wax will melt into the wood and be nearly impossible to clean at a certain point. I recommend a high-quality plastic or silicone spoon, or even a few sturdy stainless steel stirring spoons if you can find them.

**Silicone molds** for your wax might be needed, depending on the format of your candles. We'll talk more about the types of candles here soon, but if you plan on doing wax melts or shaped candles, you'll need molds. Don't go overboard and buy hundreds of molds you'll never use; on the other hand, be careful not to buy too few, too. You don't want your production slowed down because you only have 2 or 3 of a popular mold type.

A **scale** is absolutely essential. While I've encouraged you to save money where you can, this is something that you really don't want to skimp on. If you have enough in the budget, spend the extra money to get a digital scale. It makes it much easier to be precise, which is important when you're making candles in bulk.

## Other Helpful Items for Your Workspace

A **microwave** is a great tool for heating water, cleaning your jugs, and more. I use mine constantly, though it's more of a 'nice thing to have' in your production area than an essential item.

A **waste bin** big enough to fit a day's trash into. Keep in mind that you're going to be throwing away a lot as you go through packaging materials, so a tiny trash can just isn't going to cut it.

A **drainage bucket**. If you're even considering pouring molten wax down the drain, hold it right there! As soon as that hot wax hits water, it's going to solidify and back up your drains. A bucket for any excess drainage wax you have is essential. Again, it doesn't have to be expensive – a big bucket from Home Depot, for instance, is only a few dollars and will provide you plenty of room.

**Table covers** might seem unnecessary, but even a small amount of dirt, dust, or general junk getting into your wax can ruin your final product. To save yourself time and hassle, invest in a few table covers for your workspace, and change them out regularly.

For my workspace, especially when I started, I would lay a sheet of wax paper over the space to protect it. I could pull it up and replace it when I spilled wax, it wouldn't damage the table under, and it was relatively inexpensive. I also bought this in bulk at my local restaurant supply store.

A **wick trimmer** (or several) and wick sizing templates are both very important. I like to have several templates sort of scattered about, so I never have to hunt for the right size or details.

## Candle Supplies You'll Need

What kinds of candles do you want to create? The type of candles you wish to make will determine the types of molds, wax, and wicks you'll be using. Your particular product will dictate the supplies you'll need, but this section will give you a rough example of what to look for when you're shopping around and pricing things out.

If you're going to be making tea lights, or using them as samples (which I recommend), **tea light cups** are going to be essential. I recommend glass, aluminum, or polycarbonate. While these might be a little more expensive, they are going to be the easiest to use and will last the longest.

Obviously, you're going to need **wax**. We'll talk about the different types of wax soon, but make sure you check the quality and the ingredients in the wax you're buying before you purchase it in bulk. In fact, I encourage you to always buy a smaller amount and make test candles before investing. There is nothing like ordering pounds and pounds of a product just to discover it was mislabeled or poorly represented, and you're stuck with large quantities of a sub-par product.

**Wicks** are another obvious necessity. I like using primed (pre-waxed) wicks, but you may have a preference for another type, and that's okay.

If you want **color** in your candles, you'll need either color chips or a liquid concentrate to achieve that. Going with a higher quality color is going to result in a better final product, so keep that in mind when you're shopping around.

**Fragrances** are tricky, and it's best to take it a step at a time. Believe me, it's easy to go overboard and buy everything that sounds like it will smell great only to end up with it sitting unused on your shelves (fully organized and labeled, hopefully).

Try to purchase only what you know you're going to use at first. You can slowly add in more as you continue to grow and expand, but these little expenses can add up quickly.

**Sustainers** (the small metal weight that holds the wick in place) are essential. Also, you'll need containers to put your final products in. Your containers will be determined by what type of candles you're going to make, so don't pull the trigger on a big purchase until you have a good idea of what your final product will be. We will talk more about containers in a later chapter, but it's a good idea to start thinking about what you want your product to look like when it's presented to your customers.

**Safety stickers** might seem silly and unnecessary, but a safety sticker on the bottom of a candle or a package is important. This small addition will tell your customers that you really value their safety and that you're a legitimate business, not just someone doing this for a hobby. It's the little details that will really show your professionalism. You can purchase generic safety stickers many places online, usually in bulk. We're going to talk more about safety more in the next section.

An **apron** to protect your clothes, or multiple ones so you don't have to do laundry so often. I personally cycle through several aprons, all made of sturdy material. If I splash wax on myself, I don't want to worry about it seeping through to my clothes or burning me.

## Safety Should Be Your Priority

In addition to safety for your customers, I cannot stress enough that your own personal safety comes first. There are many hazardous elements to consider. You will be working with hot wax, open flames, and more. If this business is a side hustle for you at first, you also may be working nights, weekends, and you could find yourself very tired while you're pouring candles.

**Alertness:** Try not to work when you're so exhausted that you can't keep your eyes open. This is dangerous, and you're asking for a mistake at best. Even if you need to take a few minutes to get up, walk around your workspace, and stretch some, staying alert is better than making a mistake that will cost you the whole batch of candles you're pouring, destroy your entire workspace, or cause you bodily harm.

**Open flames:** Always keep open flames away from each other, and away from anything that could

37

catch on fire. It's easy to stop taking candle safety seriously when you first start creating them because you can become desensitized to them – but keep in mind that this is still an open flame that could burn your workspace down in an instant.

**Equipment checks:** If you're going with some second-hand equipment (which I encourage, don't get me wrong), make sure to inspect all of your cords for frayed edges or torn wires. Just a bit of exposed wiring could spark, creating major issues.

**Work smart:** Do all you can to work wisely and avoid accidents. One accident could set production back days or weeks. One little mistake can add up to hundreds or thousands of dollars in loss. Safety should be the most important thing to you.

# CHAPTER 3: TYPES OF WAX

By now, you should have an idea of the tools you need, what your space is going to look like, and how everything will be set up. Now, we're going to spend a few chapters talking about your process.

Learning and knowing your process is going to be the most important thing for your business, especially starting out. As we spend the next section discussing details of the process, make sure you become a pro at this yourself before you try to expand your business. Sometimes new start-ups want to hire someone right away to help with production, and that can be a good thing. An extra set of hands makes everything go faster, after all, and the more candles you make, the more you can sell, and the better your business will be doing – right?

Sort of.

Someday in the future, you might need to hire someone to mix and pour candles for you. Someday soon, maybe, if you're lucky – or good! But right now, starting out, you should focus on learning every aspect of your process and becoming an expert at it. This way, you can properly teach your new worker when you hire them, as well as make the best choices when you're buying your supplies. After all, you won't know what is best until you use it yourself.

This is the biggest reason why so much of my book is dedicated to knowing your process and learning properly. The more you understand the process, the better a business owner you're going to be.

First up? Arguably the most important part of any candle: wax!

Maybe you've already worked a lot with a certain type of wax and had not considered trying other types. Let me share my hard-earned wisdom with you; there are actually a lot of things to consider when it comes to candle wax.

The wax that you use in your candle matters. A lot. I would argue that the type and quality of wax you purchase is the most important thing, actually. It can also be the most overwhelming because there are so many choices from so many vendors. How do you go about choosing just one?

At a certain point, you probably won't have to choose 'just one.' You can eventually offer a variety of candles with a variety of waxes at different price points for your customers. However, I encourage you to start with just one type of wax as you build your business. Learn the ins and outs of melting, pouring, and burning that product until you feel completely comfortable with it before you tackle the next one.

Something to keep in mind? The type of wax you purchase is going to attract a specific customer. Soy wax is going to appeal to a different person than paraffin wax, while another person will like beeswax the best for their own reasons.

Knowing your target market and what they like is important.

Unsure of who your target market is? That's okay. You don't have to be there yet – we're going to talk soon about marketing, packaging, and who you can sell your candles to – but it's certainly something you need to keep in the front of your mind as you go through this process.

Alright, I'm done preaching! You understand why wax is so important. Let's dive in.

## Soy Wax

Soy wax is the newest and hottest (no pun intended) wax on the market now. That sounds weird, right? After all, people have been making and burning candles for years. Not with soy, they haven't.

Soy wax as a candle product was brought to market in the early 1990s, and just as the name suggests, it's a completely natural alternative to the very common paraffin (discussed below, stay tuned) wax that is widely available.

One of the many reasons that soy wax is so desirable right now is that it has been marketed incredibly well. In addition, it's just a really excellent, natural product all around. Soy wax is clean burning, doesn't release potentially dangerous chemicals into the air, and has the longest burn time of any commercially available wax. For example, soy wax can burn 30 to 50 percent longer than a common paraffin candle. That means a 7-ounce fully soy wax candle can burn for up to 45 hours total. That's a long time.

As the name suggests, soy is made from soybeans. Soy wax is not a byproduct of anything else, but made intentionally for candles. After the soy is harvested, cleaned, and de-hulled, it is rolled into flakes and the oil is extracted from those flakes. To put it very technically for a moment, during the hydrogenation process, the fatty acids within the soy become saturated. This saturation is what causes the melting point of the oil to rise, leaving the product – or, wax – solid at room temperature.

Soy seems like the obvious choice, right? It burns long, it's a natural product, and consumers are flocking to it because it is the newest, 'healthiest' form of wax on the market!

Well, slow down a minute, because there are downsides, too.

In my experience, soy wax is the second most expensive wax on the market right now, so keep that in mind when you're first starting out. Is it worth it? That's going to depend on your ideal consumer and their needs, so only you as the business owner can decide. But you need to make an educated decision. Soy candles continue to grow in popularity, and I wouldn't be surprised to see the market dominated by them within the next 5-10 years.

Soy wax is also softer than the traditional paraffin counterpart. This means it melts at a lower temperature, which is great, but when stored in very warm conditions, it can melt on its own. I don't think I need to tell you how not great that is.

Some manufacturers have decided to go half-and-half with the process, adding paraffin into their soy compounds for a variety of reasons: stability, the longevity of the fragrance, the 'throw' of fragrance (how far you can smell your candle when it's burning), and more. This is an option for you, but make sure you spend plenty of time finding a good ratio for the types of candles you want to make.

## Palm Wax

Following up the increasingly popular soy wax is palm wax, which is made very similarly to soy. It is also a newer wax, and it's the most firm wax we have on the list. Some have even described palm wax as brittle, which is probably fair. Because of the structure and density of palm wax, it is the perfect choice for votive or pillar candles. It also has a relatively high melting point, so your votive candles won't melt in shipping.

Like soy, palm wax has a long burn time, which is great. It also needs a relatively high fragrance load (the amount of fragrance you put into the wax) for the candle, but it isn't so high that it should deter you from considering palm wax.

The biggest issue with palm wax is the sourcing. You may or may not be aware of this, but there is a huge concern right now about palm oil and how it is sourced. Nearly 90% of the palm oil produced right now comes from the forests of Malaysia, and the deforestation there is incredibly heartbreaking. In addition, there are countless reports of labor violations, unfair work conditions, and more – all to produce palm oil and, to a lesser extent, palm wax. This may give you pause personally, and also may do so for your customers.

I'm not going to judge you for using palm wax. It's cheaper than soy, and it's a sturdy replacement for a lot of reasons. But I suggest you find a quality, reliable supplier that isn't hurting the environment or a local community overseas. Otherwise, I cannot personally recommend palm oil.

## Paraffin Wax

This is the most common wax available. Sometimes called mineral wax or crude oil wax, paraffin wax is the cheapest wax out there. Nearly every candle that you see on a commercial shelf is made from paraffin wax, and you can purchase it almost anywhere. There are a lot of reasons to like paraffin wax.

It's cheap, for one thing. Paraffin wax is produced primarily as a byproduct of crude oil refinement, so it is going to exist whether people use it for candles or not. This makes it easy to come by.

Paraffin wax retains its color well in the long term, which is important if you're a big fan of making colored candles. Other waxes will lose their vibrancy within a short time, but paraffin will stay bright and fresh.

It also holds fragrance well – even strong fragrances, too. Other types of wax can lose potency over time, especially when it is burned once and then sits – but fragrances cling to paraffin forever. This makes it a clear choice for large commercial production, where candles sit for a long time and are sold cheaply.

Sounds perfect, right? But before you start searching for a supplier for your paraffin wax, I want you to know about some of the negatives. Many consumers, especially those looking for a high-end candle, are moving away from paraffin because it releases volatile organic compounds (or VOCs) when burned. What are VOCs?

Well, it's still a fuzzy scientific area, but it is believed that VOCs can damage the environment over time, as well as cause issues for users who burn candles in enclosed spaces. You know, like in a bedroom, an office, or a living room.

Right now the jury is still out on just how harmful burning paraffin wax can be, or if VOCs are really released at a rate that is concerning. A 2009 study done at South Carolina State University led the charge against paraffin, but the study was never published in a peer-reviewed journal, and further testing has been inconclusive at best.

Should you use paraffin? Maybe – it's certainly tempting. Again, this is a decision only you can make based on your ideal clientele, price point, and more. But be sure you're aware of the risks, and the negative outlook many consumers have, before you pull the trigger.

## Beeswax

Welcome to my absolute favorite wax – beeswax! Beeswax is thought to be the oldest form of wax for candles, and remains of beeswax candles have been found in Egyptian pyramids, suggesting that it has been around for thousands of years. Not to 'nerd out' on you, but isn't it amazing that we're still using the same methods and tools that were used so long ago?

Beeswax is a natural byproduct of the honey-making process, and no bees are harmed in the making of ethically produced beeswax. The final product of wax contains a little bit of honey, which leaves a sweet, gentle fragrance within the wax itself. The specific scent actually depends on not just the bees that produced the wax, but the type of pollen the bees preferred. Beeswax from bees that consumed wildflowers will smell different than those who consumed clover. Isn't that incredible?

Being a completely natural product, beeswax also burns completely cleanly, unlike the paraffin wax option we just talked about. There is no air pollution, and it's totally safe and even good for the environment.

However, there are some very clear downsides to beeswax, and one of them is the price. Good quality beeswax is by and far the most expensive wax you're going to find on the market, and for good reason. Taking the raw honeycombs and creating wax from it is a long, drawn-out process, and that doesn't even begin to include how much money and time it takes to raise your own bees, to get to the point where you can harvest the honeycombs.

Another downside for some, in addition to the completely justified high price, is the fact that beeswax cannot be scented. It won't properly hold or mix any sort of fragrance you want to put in it, so what you see is what you get. Some suggest using essential oils to scent beeswax, but I have not yet found a successful method to do so. Going without fragrance can limit your creativity a lot, and not everyone wants a candle that smells only vaguely like flowers or honey.

Is beeswax great? Absolutely! But I don't personally use it for the downsides listed above. You, however, certainly can. Think about your target market, your startup costs, and what you want to get out of your business. If beeswax fits your brand and your dream, go for it!

## Candle Gel Wax

I'm going to be honest with you and admit that candle gel wax is my least favorite choice. It's also not technically a wax – it's a gel wax, which is basically a blend of oils and resins. If you remember those very popular kitschy candles from a few years ago with floating solid pieces in them, like tiny wax shoes or lipsticks, you've probably seen candle gel wax.

To be fair, let's talk first about some of the positive or unique aspects of gel wax. For one, candle gel wax is very interesting in that, when solid, it is completely clear. That's pretty neat, and it allows someone creative to do a lot with their final product. Throw some flower petals in, leaves, glitter – whatever you want, it can be done.

The product is also very good at holding fragrance and color, which is a big plus for those using candle gel wax. If you're considering this gel wax for your candle making, be sure to pay close attention to your supplier and test a sample first. Why? Because not all products will solidify clear – some have a little bit of an off color to them, which of course is perfectly fine if you're going to color your candles. But if you're going for a completely clear candle, make sure you order the right product.

A big downside to candle gel wax is that it is technically made from the same byproduct that paraffin wax is made from. If you have consumers avoiding paraffin wax for health or environmental reasons, they will be avoiding your candle gel wax, too. Again, carefully consider what your final product will be and who will be purchasing it before you make these decisions.

## Coconut Wax

Did you know coconut wax for candles was even a thing? It's relatively unknown right now, but it's quickly growing in popularity because it has many of the benefits of soy or palm wax. For one thing, coconut wax is incredibly slow-burning, so candles that are made from it last longer.

Coconut wax also has an incredible scent throw. Coconut wax can hold more fragrance than nearly any other wax on the market right now, which means it smells stronger for longer when you burn it. Even if you're not burning it, coconut wax has a scent throw that many consumers find pleasant.

Finally, many environmentalists find it ideal. Just like soy and palm wax, coconut wax is very clean burning. There is no negative environmental impact, it won't leave behind a soot residue, and zero studies have found any VOCs released when it burns. It's also believed to be one of the most ethically produced waxes, as coconuts do not need pesticides or fertilizer to grow, and the trees do not need to be destroyed to be harvested.

Downsides of coconut wax include the price, which still tends to be higher than traditional wax, and allergen concerns. While there is little evidence on whether those who have a coconut allergy can or cannot handle burning coconut wax, many people avoid it just in case.

Coconut wax is also the least-known wax, so many people won't understand or appreciate the distinction.

## What's in a Blend?

So, let's say that you like the stability of paraffin wax, the sustainability of soy, and you want to merge the two. No problem. That's absolutely something you can do!

Mixing waxes to produce a blend is very common, and it's a great way to produce a product that is unique or perfectly suited for your needs. If you need something more stable than just soy for a pillar candle, you can mix it with coconut or palm wax to produce a solid product.

Finding the right ratios for each product is going to be a series of trial and error, plus figuring out what others do. When I mix soy and paraffin, I use 2 parts soy to 3 parts paraffin (so, for every 2 ounces of soy wax, I add 3 ounces of paraffin wax), which produces a highly scented, sturdy candle. What you are using your mix for will dictate the perfect amounts for each type of candle.

Always remember, however, to thoroughly test your mixes before bringing them to market. Don't just burn one candle halfway, but burn several completely through with all of the scents you want to try before selling them. Sometimes mixing or settling issues occur, and you could be in for a surprise—and you definitely don't want your customers to be!

## Much to Consider

There is a lot to consider when choosing your wax, so take your time and do your research. When designing a candle, make sure to consider the fragrance load a wax is going to need to smell good, the density of the wax, and the melting point, as well as the price.

While this choice you make now isn't make or break – no one is saying you can't switch in six months; after all, it's your business – it is important to do your research and feel confident with your choices.

After deciding on some wax choices, or at least narrowing it down, it's time to get into part two of knowing your process completely. That is, what makes a good wick good – and how to pick what wick is best for your candle business.

# CHAPTER 4: TYPES OF WICKS AND CANDLES

Are wicks for a candle important?

You'd be surprised. When thinking about making your candles to market and sell to others, wicks might seem like the least important thing. The packaging, the types of candles, and the wax are all more important, right?

Well, no. Wicks deserve their own consideration, too. While they might not seem as important of an item as the container you place your candles in or the wax that burns, wicks serve an important function. And without the proper wick, all you have is a jar full of wax.

A wick's main purpose is to provide the fuel for the candle itself. A wick that burns too hot or too fast will tunnel through a candle without ever touching the wax along the edges. A wick that burns too slow won't melt the wax fast enough, creating an issue where very little of the scent is released.

I could literally write this book on wick types alone, and it probably wouldn't be long enough. There are hundreds of wicks on the market right now. But I would like to take a moment, in the interest of helping you know your business inside and out, to talk about the most common ones you will run into, and how to determine what type of wick you should use for each type of candle.

## Braided vs. Twisted

The first thing you're probably going to notice is that there are two main types of wick construction: braided wicks and twisted wicks.

A braided wick is the most common wick type you're going to see when you start making candles, and for good reason. Braided, knitted, or plaited fibers encourage a slower, more steady burn. This slower burn is going to help your candle last longer, and the heat will reach and incorporate more of the wax so that less is wasted. This is obviously the ideal situation.

Twisted wicks, on the other hand, are a much faster, hotter burn. This is because their construction is much looser, allowing more air in between the fibers. Twisted wicks are ideal for a fast-burning, thin candle – like the kind of candle you would use on a birthday cake. For a larger candle, however, twisted wicks aren't what you are looking for.

Twisted wicks generally are also cheaper and lower quality than a braided or plaited wick. In general, I would not advise using twisted wicks (unless, of course, you're making birthday candles!).

## Common Types of Wicks

This section will cover the most common types of wicks you will see when you start shopping. Again, there are many types you will run into, but these are the ones you will find at most suppliers.

## Flat Wicks

There is a good chance that the flat wick is going to be the wick type you find the most, and for the best price. Flat wicks are normally knitted or plaited, and generally made from three separate bundles of wick fibers wound together tightly.

The benefit of flat wicks is that they have a self-trimming effect. As the wick burns, it tends to curl into itself, meaning that your customers don't have to trim their own wicks. This extra step seems small, but it is a nice benefit that most people just don't think about.

## Cored Wicks

A cored wick is a type of braided wick that has two very distinct parts – the inner 'core', and the outer fibers. This structure ensures that the wick doesn't bend into itself, like a flat or square wick, and instead stands upright.

The most common core materials you'll see in a cored wick include tin, zinc, cotton, and even paper. The material in the core will determine how stiff the wick stands and how well it burns.

Cored wicks are often rounded in appearance and best used for pillar candles, votives, and devotional lights, but they also work well in jar candles. Unsurprisingly, however, cored wicks tend to run on the more expensive end.

**Square Wicks**

A square wick is similar to a flat wick in that it basically trims itself – a huge benefit for your customers. A square wick is a little more robust than a flat wick, however, and has a more rounded appearance. Square wicks were originally used for beeswax candles because of their sturdy construction and slow burn, but they can be used for any candle type.

The biggest benefit of a square wick is that they prevent wick clogging. If you're struggling with maintaining a flame for the duration of your candle's life, you might be experiencing wick clogging, which is when the debris of any kind gets 'stuck' in the wick. Pigments and wick trimmers are the two biggest causes of wick clogging. With square wicks, you have zero risk.

**Wooden Wicks**

Wooden wicks are my personal favorite type of wicks, at least when it comes to burning candles in my own life, on my own time. A good quality wooden wick should be sturdy. When it's burned, it should produce a lovely crackling noise – like the sound of a fireplace – along with a flickering, dancing flame.

Wooden wicks can be 100% wood or mixed with other materials like cotton. These can be purchased as thin single-ply, multi-layered, curved, or even in unique decorative shapes. Wooden wicks are expensive, but they are impressive-looking, and a really great look for a higher-quality candle or a special occasion.

**Wait, There Are More Wicks?!**

Yes! Believe it or not, there are more types of wicks than just the common ones I included in the previous section. Some candles have cores, which come in a variety of materials for different purposes. Yet some wicks have no cores. I'm going to briefly go over the other wick options for you; but as always, be sure to do your own thorough research on each type of wick that you're considering using (and the manufacturer making them) before you take the plunge. Testing is also essential, which we'll talk about soon.

**Performa coreless wicks** are flat-braided and made completely out of cotton. These wicks are sturdy and will not bend, but will need to be trimmed. They also have a bright, strong flame, which can be very visually appealing.

**HTP wicks**, or high-tension paper wicks, are an excellent choice for nearly any type of wax. These reinforced wicks remain sturdy and tall during their burning time, but also self-trim, so your customers won't have that hassle.

**LX wicks** are also coreless, just like the Performa, and are braided flat. These will bend more than the Performa coreless wicks, but they are engineered to reduce smoke, soot buildup (no more mushrooming!), and afterglow. These work best with soy or paraffin wax, and are good choices for pillar candles or container candles.

**RRD series wicks** are similar to the LX wicks, and are rounded, cotton-cored braided candle wicks that are specifically designed to increase fuel flow to the flame. This produces a great burn and fragrance throw for any candle, and is generally very stable. RRD series wicks also do not clog, which is especially great if you're looking to create a highly-pigmented votive or container candle.

**Zinc wicks** are a cotton-braid wick that has an inner zinc core. Have you ever trimmed a candle to encounter a small metal wire in the middle of the wick? It was probably a zinc-core wick. The zinc gives maximum rigidity and strength to keep the wick straight as the candle burns. Like LX wicks, these discourage mushrooming from carbon buildup. These are cooler burning and recommended for paraffin wax candles such as containers, votives, small novelty candles, and floating candles.

Finally, we have **CD series wicks**, which are another coreless wick that is braided. CD series wicks, however, are flat, and woven with a paper filament that is designed for maximum burn and a consistent rate of burn. CD series wicks are best for waxes that are more solid, like coconut wax.

## How Do I Choose the Right Size Wick for My Candles?

This is a very common question that those new to the candle-making business struggle with. How can you choose the right wick size for your candles? There are so many choices, right? Thankfully, it's easier to figure out than just using trial and error – although that is part of the process – but it's also more complicated than just telling you a flat number.

Once you have selected a supplier for your candle-making supplies, look for any charts they have. Their specific recommendations will be the best to go by, because the company that makes the wick is going to have the best idea of what burns well for what size. However, make sure you are still testing because each type of wax, blend of wax, or size of container is going to have different needs.

Below is an example of a chart for container candles, and the types of wicks you should be using for each size and wax type. In general, the wider the diameter of your candle, the larger your wick should be. The tab size refers to the small metal tab that is used to anchor the wick, if you end up creating your own. This is just a guide, and as you progress, you will find what works best for you. In fact, if you produce several different types, you may want to create your own similar chart to keep things organized.

| Candle Size | Wick Type | Wax Type | Tab Size | Coating Type |
| --- | --- | --- | --- | --- |
| 1-2" | CD-3 | Gel | 20x9mm | 210° |
| 1-2" | 34-40 Zinc | Paraffin | 20mm | High Melting Point |
| 1-2" | RRD-29 nst 2 | Vegetable Wax | 20mm | High Melting Point |
| 2-3" | HZL 38 C | Gel | 20x9mm | 210° |
| 2-3" | LX-14 | Paraffin | 20mm | High Melting Point |
| 2-3" | RRD-40 nst 2 | Vegetable Wax | 20mm | High Melting Point |
| 3-4" | HTP-105 | Gel | 20x9mm | 210° |
| 3-4" | CD-16 | Paraffin | 20mm | High Melting Point |
| 3-4" | RRD-47 nst 2 | Vegetable Wax | 20mm | High Melting Point |
| 4"+ | 60-44-18 Cotton | Paraffin | 20mm | High Melting Point |
| 4"+ | 2 RRD-34 nst 2 | Vegetable Wax | 20mm | High Melting Point |

A little overwhelmed? It's okay! The first time you buy wicks you might feel overwhelmed – like you have no idea what you're doing or buying – but I promise, it will get easier. At some point you're going to reference this chart and realize you already know every type of wick above, and understand why these sizes matter.

Alright, we've talked about wax. We've talked about wicks. What's next in your journey to knowing your business inside out?

The structure of your actual product. That is, candles! Let's dive into the world of candle shapes and types, and see what we can learn.

## The Types of Candles

There is a good chance that at this point in the book, you already have an idea of the type of candles you want to make. That's great! But there is a lot to think about, and you've got a lot of options. It also doesn't hurt to keep multiple ideas in mind – you don't just have to sell one type of candle, after all. As you grow and expand, multiple types of candles may be in your future.

So, what are the differences in candles, and how do you choose what wax to make them from? There's a good probability that you're already familiar with most of these types, so I'll keep this section short. Let's just touch on the varieties of candles you have to choose from, and how to pick the best candles for your business.

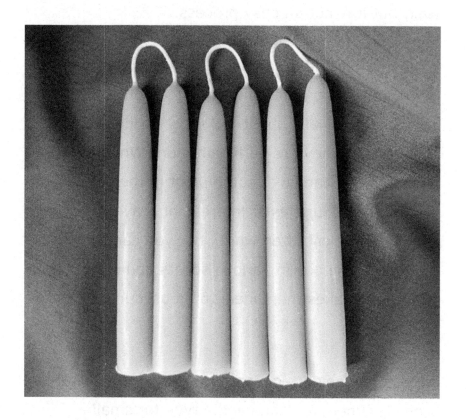

**Dipped candles** are unique in that they are a long, thin shape that is fairly distinctive. These are also an older style of candle, so they're not quite as popular as some other choices we've got here on our list. These are quite a process to make successfully, as dipping your candle repeatedly in wax is how the sturdy, thin shape is achieved. The best waxes to create dipped candles include paraffin or beeswax. You want something sturdy but pliable. You may be able to create a dipped candle with another type of wax, but it is not an easy process.

**Votive candles** are immediately recognizable. Short and sturdy, but taller than tea lights, votive candles are usually about 1-2 inches wide and 2-3 inches high. They are fairly common: Who hasn't seen a votive candle at some point in their life? They are found in churches or in areas of prayer, votive candles are most often white, but you can also find them sold in a box in various scents and colors. Their small size makes them ideal to be used in decorative glass holders.

Because they are generally a low price point, these aren't a super common candle type for small businesses to make – but there isn't anything that says you can't! If these are candles you feel passionately about, or that your target market buys, then you could absolutely consider offering them. Remember, however, that things associated with religion or prayer can be a sacred or sensitive subject. Be careful with your wording and proper terminology, so as not to accidentally offend your market. (The same holds true for devotional candles.)

Most waxes work well for a votive candle – including soy, beeswax, palm oil, and wax blends. You want to avoid anything too soft.

**Container candles** are the most common type of candles small businesses offer, in my opinion. These candles are in, well, containers of various types, and they are easy to make and easy to burn. Most people prefer container candles because they have little mess and are easy to move around a home or business.

Container candles can be made from any type of wax, because the wax does not have to hold up under its own weight. These are the easiest to make, the easiest to sell, and the easiest to personalize in order to get your own logo and stamp on them. I highly recommend starting with container candles, at least at first. It's just easier.

**Rolled candles** are an option, but can be a bit of a pain, so beware. The only wax you can create a rolled candle from is beeswax, because it comes in long sheets that you roll up. This is for a very specific target market, so be careful making this choice and do your research first. These candles are beautiful, long-lasting, and smell great, but again— for a specific market.

**Pillar candles** are also common, and as the name suggests, are shaped like a pillar – long and tall and sturdy. These are probably the second most common variety of candles and certainly have a place in many homes.

You can use wax blends, beeswax, palm wax, and paraffin to create pillar candles that burn well and look beautiful. I do not encourage you to try pillar candles with soy or gel wax, however, as these softer materials will melt too quickly, leading to a fiery, dangerous mess.

**Wax melts** aren't technically a candle, I suppose, but they do deserve a mention here. You may have noticed their popularity, and there are some boutique varieties. Wax melts are little squares of colored, highly-scented wax that go into a special warmer. Wax tarts are shaped like tiny round tarts instead of squares. Wax melts are growing in popularity, especially with parents who are concerned about open flames near their children or pets.

Melts can be made from nearly any wax, though I recommend staying away from gel. Soy and palm wax are especially suited for melts, but paraffin will also work just fine. If you're going to be offering melts, the good news is that you don't have to think about the type of wick needed.

# CHAPTER 5: EVERYTHING YOU NEED TO KNOW ABOUT SCENTS

The fragrances you offer can help you stand out from your competition. Choosing the best scent for your target market and your brand is going to make or break your business, so it's important to thoughtfully and carefully select your scents and product line. Anyone can produce a vanilla candle– so what makes yours better?

As you read this section, think about the scents you love, and what your target market will love. Be unique. Be creative. If you try to create your scent line too generically, you're not going to have anyone actually interested in buying your products!

## Smell, Smell, Smell

Before you invest in gallons of a fragrance that you're not sure you will like, I encourage you to buy several samples. Any decent fragrance company will offer small sample packages that will let you smell something before you invest.

Think about what your target market likes, and go with that. You're absolutely allowed to sell common candle fragrances (hello vanilla), or those that appeal to a mass audience, but always keep in mind what you can offer to make your business unique, or what you would want in a candle. Is it lemongrass and green tea, with a hint of honey? Maybe fresh coffee beans, cream, and a touch of sweetness? What fragrances can you combine to get there?

You don't have to stay inside the box, so to speak. Get creative; check out all of your options. If you're not sold on a scent, don't force it – sometimes, the description of the scent sounds better than the scent itself smells. And sometimes, it just won't work with your nose chemistry.

## Quality Matters

I'm going to encourage you from my own personal experience to put a lot of thought into not just how you choose your scents but also the supplier you buy from. Buying a cheap-smelling scent is going to make your candle smell – well, cheap – no matter how expensive the wax is.

Quality is better than quantity, and your fragrance is not a corner you want to cut, especially if you're marketing to a higher quality demographic. I know that up until this point, I have encouraged you to buy the cheaper product, try the cheaper tool, and get a lot of your core tools second-hand. But in the fragrance department? Don't skimp; take your time and buy a quality product.

Quality fragrance literally will make or break your final product – especially in the world of making a name for yourself in the candle-making landscape. Believe me!

## Don't Be Afraid to Ask Around

Not sure what you like? Ask a few friends to come over (hopefully they're in your target market) and get them to smell your scents, too. Do they think it smells cheap, like hotel soap? Does it smell high-end? Would they buy a cayenne-lime candle, or is that a little too out there, even for them?

This kind of feedback is so important for a new business, and you're doing yourself a disservice if you don't take advantage of all the resources available to you. This includes your friends and family, who certainly just want to see you succeed – and likely will be among your first customers.

If you can't get everyone together in the same room, consider making small candles of your top scents and sending them off for testing. I'll talk about this again at the end of the book, but this feedback can really help boost your confidence and give you important information about your final product.

## Create Thoughtful Scents

There is a subtle art to scent creation, and it can be fascinating. In the very first chapter, I talked about how closely scent is tied with memory and feelings.

In fact, t's literally wired into our brain to feel a certain way about a scent, and candles bring that scent right there. When you're crafting a line of scents, I want you to be thoughtful and purposeful with them.

If you're struggling, tie everything back to something. If you're creating your winter collection, maybe it triggers your feelings on the first snow of the year, or drinking a cup of hot chocolate as a child after coming in from a long morning of playing in the backyard. Perhaps it's the smell of crisp leaves in the fall, when the weather becomes just cool enough for a sweater, but not so cold you need to turn on your heater.

As you're smelling potential scents, ask yourself if it would be a scent you would find pleasing if you walked into someone's house? Would you find it appealing as a perfume? Is this something that you would get tired of burning for 40 hours?

I recommend that each scent you create mean something to you. Creating from the heart and crafting a scent that is important to you will absolutely show in the final product, and your customers will appreciate it.

If you really put your heart and soul into creating a unique fragrance line – who knows? You may even develop a signature scent!

## Your Library of Scents

Consider what kinds of scents you want to offer. You should have two categories: a core library, which are fragrances you offer year round. Then it's important to have special scents—I'll call them seasonal or special-occasion scents. You really need both kinds of scents. Customers want the old standbys available whenever they need them, but they also like to try something new. So give them both!

## Creating Your Core Library

Every good candle business should have a core library of scents. These are reliable, standard scents that everyone can identify as part of your brand, that will burn well year-round. Choose scents that your target market will love, and that you love, too. After all, you'll be smelling these a lot!

These scents should not be seasonal at all. Consider scents like cookies and cream, fresh-baked pie, coffee house, aqua dreams. Whatever you choose, these are going to stick with you.

Research popular year-round fragrances. But, as mentioned before, create scents that mean something to you. Scents are powerful, so put lots of time and effort into these core scents. Your entire line is going to be built around these choices, and it's really going to define who you are as a business.

## Seasonal Offers: Highly Encouraged

I highly encourage you to do seasonal product lines, or product lines based on holidays – or both! Changing your inventory is going to encourage people to come back to your site, and everyone loves a good holiday scent or design. Again, this is also a great way to set yourself apart from some of your competition, something you should always be thinking about.

**Spring scents** should remind you of rebirth, of new beginnings, of fresh joy and hope. With spring comes longer days, new flowers, new growth. We all have a chance for a new start in the spring.

Spring also has several holidays, including Easter and Mother's Day. Playing off these holidays and offering specific candles, like marshmallow and candy scents for Easter or flowers and wine for Mother's Day, can bring a lot of extra revenue for those looking to give gifts.

**Summer** is full of hot days, freshly cut grass, BBQs outside, and spending time with the family. Try to think about your favorite summer activity, and how to put it in a candle. Is it walking outside on Saturday when the sun is shining, the grass smells freshly cut, and the flowers are in full bloom? Or is it hiking outside, hearing nature all around you, smelling the woods and the trees?

Summer holidays include Memorial Day and July 4th, and often bring memories of backyard parties, swimming in pools, and eating burnt hot dogs in the shade of a tree. What can you bring to the table, in candle form, that reminds people of the summer and these holidays? Blueberry pie? Root beer? Lemonade?

**Fall** is my personal favorite season, and I know I'm not alone. Crisp leaves, the first snow, cooler nights, sitting by a bonfire – all scents that bring fall to mind. Pumpkin spice is also a popular theme, but apple cider and pies also apply.

Thanksgiving and Halloween are also huge holidays in the US, and there are plenty of candle scents you can create that remind people of these beloved holidays and traditions. Stuffing, cranberry sauce, turkey, candy, spooky nights. Put some time into creating a unique scent that takes you to a specific time.

**Winter** is long and dark for many, and most people are searching for scents that make them feel comforted. Warm flannel, warm spices, and the smell of fire and family. Spicy, woody scents are perfect for wintertime – no one really wants to smell fresh flowers in the dead of winter. It just reminds you of what you can't have! Fresh bread and baked goods are always a winner for winter, too.

Christmas and New Year's are also during winter. Mulled wine, sweet ham, and Christmas cookies are all great scent choices. Celebratory scents for New Year's to ring in the moment are not just welcomed but encouraged! What scent reminds you of a party with all your friends, of fresh beginnings, of a new start?

## Finding a Balance

Your goal should be to find a balance somewhere between 'perfect for everyone' and 'completely out there.' Try scent combinations your competitors don't have; don't just imitate what is working for them.

Your core line should be something that everyone can love, all the time. Your seasonal or holiday lines should bring people to a moment in their lives that they are happy to revisit, something that reminds them of this moment in time. Finding a balance is going to take time and a lot of consideration to your target market, but once you've hit that sweet spot, you're going to find success!

# CHAPTER 6: THE VERY BASICS OF CANDLE MAKING

As I mentioned earlier, I assume you've made a candle before, and that you understand the basics of heating wax and pouring candles. However, since it is so important that you understand your process completely, we will touch on this for a chapter. Feel free to skip this section, though you may learn something new. Even if you're an experienced chandler, I encourage you to skim through it, at least.

We will start with four types of candles. This is not a comprehensive guide to making every type of candle, start to finish – think of it more as a collection of good tips and best practices to follow to ensure you've got this down to a science.

If you have never poured a candle before (first of all, wow, that takes a lot of guts to start a candle business without making a candle), that's okay, too. This should be an excellent introduction for you, and help you avoid some trial and error going forward.

I'll give you a checklist for each type, followed by step-by-step instructions. Let's make some candles together!

## Container Candles

I've talked before about how much I love container candles, so it's no surprise I'm starting here!

*You will need:*
Wax
Wicks
Wick bar
Wick setter, straw, or Bic pen

Fragrance (optional)

Dye (optional)

Pouring pot

Double boiler (see Ch. 2)

Thermometer

Stirring spoons

Containers

Paper towels

Glue gun

Alright, so the first step is to weigh out the amount of wax you're going to need. So how much wax should you use for the containers you have? Look at the containers you want to fill; their capacity should be printed on the bottom of the container (in ounces). Or, if it's an unmarked jar or container, fill the container with water, then pour it into a measuring cup to get the ounces per each container. Once you know how many total ounces of wax you will need, drop that amount of wax into your double boiler (don't overfill), and melt down the wax.

The ideal temperature is probably going to be between 170-180°, but this will depend on what wax you're using, obviously. If you're unsure, look up the suppliers' instructions. Once you've hit your temperature and everything is well melted, you're going to put any additives in it.

I recommend adding fragrance oil first, before anything else. A general rule of thumb is 1 ounce of fragrance oil per pound of wax, but each type of wax is going to have a different fragrance load. Choose the amount that is appropriate for the volume of wax you're working with and the type of wax.

Measure and add your dye. Again, this is going to depend on the type of dye you're using (blocks melt fastest when chopped into pieces), and what type of wax you're using. Mix thoroughly until the dye is completely incorporated with the wax.

Once your fragrance and dye are both well mixed, test your color on a paper towel. In your double boiler your wax is going to look very dark, but this might not be the color it will come out. Drop a tiny amount of wax (be careful, it's hot) onto a paper towel or even a paper plate. Allow the wax to harden completely, and you should get a better idea of what color your final candle will be.

Alright, your wax is ready. Let's get our containers ready, too.

Note: You absolutely can preheat your containers, and you will get a more consistent, better quality finished product. Some home candle makers choose to use their oven, but if you are not in a space where you can do that, a heat gun on the lowest setting will work just fine. Be careful, because those suckers do get hot fast, and you can easily go above the target temperature of about 150 degrees. This step is optional, though, and you don't have to.

There is a tool called an EX Wick Setter that basically lets you center your wick in a container and sticks it to the bottom. That's cool, but it's not needed – you can use a straw or even the hollow part of a disassembled Bic pen.

Using a pen or a straw, insert the wick completely through with the bottom of the wick tab facing you. Place a dot of hot glue on the bottom of the wick tab, and then use the shaft to push the tab firmly into the bottom center of the container.

Okay! Now it's time to pour. Be careful and pour your hot wax slowly. Moving too fast can cause air bubbles or splashed wax, both of which are annoying at best.

Once you've poured your candles, go back to your first candle and set the wick to the center. A wick bar can be used, and they aren't very expensive – or you can use a clothespin or even a big chip clip. Anything that will sit over the candle container and hold everything centered and steady works well.

After you center the wick, leave the candles to cool and set completely before removing the wick bar or wick holder. Don't remove the wick bar too quickly, or you can upset the candle and hurt the cooling process. Do not set the candles under a cool air vent or directly in front of a fan because you want a nice, even cool from top to bottom.

Once you trim the wick and your candles have cooled, add your customized labels. Now you're ready to go!

### *Common Q:* Why Do I Have a Weird Crater?

Sometimes even the most perfectly poured candles have a strange little crater around the wick. It's just part of the cooling process, and it may require a second small pour to fill the hole and set it. Some people use a heat gun or hair dryer to even out the surface of the candle after a second pour. Don't worry, you didn't do anything wrong – this depends on the shape of your container, the temperature of the room, and a lot of other factors.

## Pillar Candles

These are very similar, but not exact, to our previous process. Pillar candles require using a candle mold.

*You will need:*

Wax

Wicks

Wick bar

Wick setter, straw, or Bic pen

Fragrance (optional)

Dye (optional)

Pouring pot

Double boiler (see Ch. 2)

Thermometer

Stirring spoons

Candle molds

Mold release

A big difference between doing pillar candles and doing container candles is that it's absolutely essential that you heat your molds first. Otherwise, you could end up with a less than desirable final product because of something called surface chilling. Heating the molds will prevent this from happening.

Use the same system as above to set your wick into the center of your mold. Some molds have a hole in the bottom to feed the wick up through; if yours does, you'll need a wick sealer or type of clay to hold the wick in place and seal off the area around the hole (otherwise, the hot wax will just pour out of the bottom). If you're using silicone mold spray, this is when you'll apply it – it should be applied every six uses or so, to help candles lift out easily and without issue.

Just like in our previous step, weigh out the amount of wax you plan to use and heat it within your double boiler. Once you hit 190°, you can add your dye and mix everything together nicely. If you're not adding anything extra to it, just heat straight to 200°.

Once you hit 200°, back your heat down to around 175° and add your fragrance. You want to avoid adding your fragrance oils at a higher temp because it can break them down or change the way they smell – not ideal!

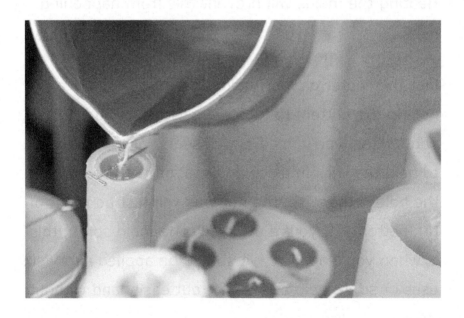

Once everything is mixed and you're at a good 175°, it's time to pour. Your wax will shrink as it cools, so leave a little room for a second pour. You should have enough wax, with this amount left out, to pour in a small cup. Label it clearly, and save it for topping off your molds.

Let your candles cool off completely – two to three hours, usually – and then reheat your remaining wax to top your candles off. Yes, this is necessary. With the cooling shrinkage, you won't get the right amount until you melt twice. Annoying, but true.

Finally, once you've cooled a second time, you can take the mold off. Trim your wicks, and you've got a successful pillar candle. It's a little more complicated than the container candle, but not by much.

## Rolled Candles

I've already expressed my love-hate relationship with beeswax. Despite the fact that I don't use it professionally, I have made rolled candles before. They're easy, and they look amazing – but as you already know, they are expensive to make, and you can't get very creative with them. Despite that, I'm going to include a brief tutorial for these, too, in case your target market is the type to gravitate to beeswax.

*You will need:*
Beeswax sheets
Primed wick
A very sharp knife
A surface you can cut on (cutting board, self-healing mat)
(Yes, that's really it!)

Lay out a single sheet on a flat surface. Along one edge, lay out a wick that is about an inch longer than the height of the sheet. I like to allow the wick to extend about 3/4 inch on each end of the sheet, and then after I'm done, I can decide which end is 'prettier' for the top. Also, this way, I know for sure my wick didn't get lost somewhere in the middle.

Place the wick at the edge of the sheet, and then roll the sheet carefully around it, about an eighth of an inch. Press firmly down on your first roll to ensure your wick is secured and everything is nice and tight.

Continue rolling your candle, going slow and steady. Heavy pressure is only needed for the very first roll. After that, a gentle, steady motion is all you should need to roll your candle up.

As you're rolling your sheet up, focus on keeping everything in line and even. You shouldn't have any bumps, waves, or misaligned edges.

Once you've hit the end of the roll, you can finish your candle. Or, if you want a thicker candle, then just add another sheet. Once you've rolled to your limit, you should be able to hold the candle in your hand and simply use the heat of your hand and gentle pressure to smooth the visible edge back into the surface of the candle.

Evaluate the candle, determine which end is going to be the top, and trim the wicks accordingly.

That's it. Really – you're done! I told you, rolled candles are very easy to make.

If you want a shorter candle, trim your wax sheets before you roll them. You can use multiple colored sheets to create a unique, almost rainbow effect, or you can trim your sheets vertically for a skinny candle. The sky is the limit!

## Wax Melts

Perhaps one of the easiest candles that you'll melt and pour, wax melts almost feel like cheating after you've struggled with a pillar candle mold that doesn't want to release or a finicky container candle. Wax melts are very popular, and you can absolutely make and sell these in your store!

*You will need:*
Double boiler
Pouring pot
Wax
Fragrance
Dye
Molds
Mold release

As with every step, melt your measured wax fully in your double boiler. Once you hit 175°, add in your fragrance oil, and then your dye. With wax melts, I find you can add a little more fragrance than a normal load because they need to be able to melt at a lower temperature. (This is why so many people think wax melts smell better.) Experiment with your exact wax type and blend to find a fragrance load that works for you.

Ready your molds, and preheat them just like a pillar candle, with a heat gun or in the oven. I like silicone molds because they are the easiest to release, and they come in lots of fun shapes. Floral melts for the summer in the shape of flowers? Yes, please!

Pour your prepared wax into the molds, and give it several hours to cool. Just like with a pillar candle, save a little after for a second pour to fill your mold up completely and give your customer all of what they ordered, not most of what they ordered.

Once the second cool has happened, pop out your melts and get them ready for packaging. In my experience, an air-tight container is best – but for just storing in your warehouse, waiting to ship, use what you like. Even a big Ziploc bag or a solid piece of Tupperware will work.

**Practice, Practice, Practice**

I recommend you practice as much as you possibly can in the early stages of your business, whenever you have some extra time. Make sure you know your process completely, and you are 100% comfortable with every aspect of heating, pouring, and making candles. Once you're rolling and you have orders coming in, you're going to have a lot less time to 'play around' in your own workshop to get things done.

Now, at the beginning, is the perfect time to try different dyes, fragrances, molds, and tools. Experiment, make use of this time, and get comfortable. After all, this is going to be your business.

# CHAPTER 7: HANDLING YOUR INVENTORY – THE NITTY-GRITTY

Since we've got some of the basics for a moment, let's talk a little about your inventory system. Primarily, that you need one – immediately. Running a business requires a lot of moving parts, and just like the storage needs we talked about previously, you're going to need to keep everything organized and tracked somewhere.

As a newbie, it can be tempting to order too many or too few of your supplies – either to ensure you're ready for any sales projection or to help cut initial costs. Finding that sweet spot will take time, but remember going forward, it's better to slightly over-order than under-order. Having a little extra on the shelf for next time is better than reaching to use something and realizing it's the very last one.

## Always Know What You Have On Hand

This is a must. Somewhere, you need to have a list of everything you have on hand at all times. At the end of a day, you need to mark what you did, what you've used, and update quantities. You never want to reach into a bin or shelf and realize you don't have enough of a product.

The good news is, keeping inventory doesn't have to be complicated or overwhelming.

When you are first starting your business, a spreadsheet kept on your computer, a tablet, or someplace like Google Sheets (included in Google Docs) is perfectly fine. As you grow, you might consider investing in specific inventory tracking software that is designed for crafters just like you working in creative businesses. Crafty Base is a popular choice, and QuickBooks is the preferred bookkeeping method for small businesses.

When you are ordering inventory to replenish your supplies, or even ordering a special batch for a specific project, it's best to over-order just a bit. I recommend ordering about 10% more than what you think you'll need. If you're making a batch of, say, 500 candles this week, be sure you have enough supplies – including wax, containers, or fragrance – for 10% extra, or 50 extra candles.

With any type of hand-made product, there are going to be mistakes or surprises. You're going to run into issues, especially at the beginning. Having this extra cushion is going to save you a ton of headache, and give you a little more confidence. Not every pour has to be perfect if you have some breathing room.

## When You're Ordering Products, Consider Lead Time

"Lead time" is the time between you placing an order and you receiving your order. Each supplier has a different lead time – some might only be a few days, others a few weeks. Make note of how much time it takes the various vendors to ship to you, so that you know how early to order your supplies. Raw materials ship differently, and you will probably find yourself purchasing from multiple places to get everything you need. This is totally normal, and I encourage you to shop around to find the best vendors for specific supplies.

The company you prefer to buy your wax from, after all, might have a terrible selection of fragrances. The company that makes the best metal tin containers may have terrible quality wicks. It happens, and don't feel like you're stuck with just one vendor or product.

If you know you're nearly out of x product, you should obviously order some – but before you hit "purchase" on that cart, look at your spreadsheet or inventory tracking system. What else are you low on that you could also use? This rolls into the next, bigger point: saving money on supplies.

## Reducing Costs When Ordering

You're going to want to find that sweet spot between having too much inventory, but not paying a lot to ship individual items. Each time you need to reorder supplies, do a check to see what else you can get from that vendor. Saving on shipping costs might seem like small potatoes in the short term, but in the long term, that money adds up, quickly.

When it comes to ordering your supplies, brand loyalty should have very little place in your business. Choose vendors to buy bulk goods from with the best cost-to-quality ratio, and make sure you're calculating shipping and lead time into it. Sure, you're saving $20 buying from one company, but if it takes two months to ship – can you wait that long?

If you're shopping around for suppliers, make sure you pay attention not just to companies that cater to hobbyists, but to true wholesale suppliers who will only (or primarily) sell to businesses. This is how you're going to get the best rates. Being a business, you're going to need more stock than a hobbyist anyway.

## Reducing Costs with Labor

When it comes to labor (the actual work of candle-making), bigger is sometimes better. Let me explain: the bigger the batches are that you can make at one time, the cheaper your labor is going to be. That's just a fact. If you have to pour 20 different batches of the same candle, you're wasting time. However, you need to judge based on your sales and business size just how big of a batch is worth it for you. If you're pouring 200 candles a day and selling 3 – well, that's not ideal.

Aim for the largest reasonable batches possible. It might seem wildly intimidating to do more than a handful of candles at a time, but by this point you know the process and the steps. It's not that much more work, and you're going to find the end results are very worth it.

# CHAPTER 8: SAFETY, OR HOW TO PROVIDE A GREAT, SAFE PRODUCT

Does this look safe to you? Absolutely not! That tree could catch on fire. But your customers might see a picture like this and decide to try it at home. Hopefully, your safety guidelines will dissuade them.

Candles can be hazardous to make and to use, so you need to be proactive about safety. This is going to sound like common sense, but hang with me for a moment. We're talking about flammable products that people are going to have sitting in their home for many, many hours. Safety should be your ultimate concern, and making sure that your candles won't hurt someone or burn a house down is incredibly important.

Safety is just as important in the first candle you pour that day to the last candle. It's important when you're thinking about your containers, your wick type and size, your wax – everything. I've seen a lot of smaller businesses make a mistake where they get lax in their production, change products or suppliers without proper testing, or simply don't take into account the many things that can go wrong.

First of all, don't assume that your customers understand how to safely burn candles. It might be common knowledge to you, someone that loves candles, but they may not understand how important candle maintenance is, burn times, etc. Consider using a safety sticker on your candle, or other safety information on your website.

Remember: It only takes one bad situation or accident to do great harm to someone or to ruin your business. At the very least, to cost you a lot of money and stress.

How can you best ensure the safety of your candles, your business, and ultimately, your customers?

If you're using the right materials, the right elements, and the right process, your customers should never have to think twice about burning the wick and smelling your candle in their air. Always keep the burning experience in your mind.

The best way you can keep your customers safe is to provide them proper burning instructions. You can't make them follow the instructions, of course, but it's your responsibility to provide them. Doing this covers you legally and ethically, so that if anything were to go wrong, you would be safe.

## Always Provide Safety Instructions

You can easily purchase a large package of generic candle-burning safety stickers on Amazon or from other wholesalers. These aren't expensive, they aren't intrusive, and they are your best 'first line of defense' against any major issues.

You should also provide your customers personalized, detailed safety instructions. Something that can be found on your website, on your sales page, or packaged with their candles. What should you include with this?

**Wick info:** Does the wick need to be kept at a quarter of an inch for best burning practice? Does wick debris need to be cleared out before every burn? Yes, to that second one – but don't assume your customers know it. Tell them.

**Burn time:** This is also a vital thing to include with each candle. Always let your customers know clearly the burn time – 4 hours, 40 hours, whatever – associated with the candle. It can make a huge difference for the user, and help prevent any dangerous situations.

**Other safety tips:** Spell out the need to place candles on a heat-resistant surface, keep them out of reach of pets or children, and never leave candles unattended.

## Warning!

To prevent fire and serious injury, Burn candle within sight. Keep away from drafts and vibrations. Keep out of reach of children and pets. Never burn candle on or near anything that can catch fire.

## Burning Instructions:

Trim wick to 5mm before lighting. Keep candle free of any foreign materials including matches and wick trimmings. Only burn the candle on a level, fire resistant surface. Do not burn the candle for more than 4 hours at a time.

Trust me; it's so important that these things are *clearly* communicated in writing. The things that seem obvious to you might not be obvious to your customers, so make sure that you have spelled it out clearly to ensure their safety and to protect yourself.

## What Should I Put My Candles IN?

Wait, what does this have to do with safety? You might be asking yourself. I understand; it seems more suited to the 'know your process' section, but hear me out.

New candle makers often want to be clever and fun with trying new and interesting containers for poured candles. A fun jar, an upcycled tin, whatever. At first glance, this seems like a great way to set yourself apart in the market and make your goods more appealing to your customers.

Please be careful. Not everything can withstand the heat of a candle.

No, really. You might look at that tiny flame and think that it's not very hot, or that it can't do much damage, but you would be wrong. Some containers get very hot to the touch when they are exposed to a constant, steady heat or flame. Some will melt when they get warm; some will warp. Others will crack or even shatter. None of these experiences you want to pass onto your customer. I promise you, they won't return to buy for a second time – and that will be the least of your worries.

So, how do you choose a container, if you're considering doing container candles?

1. Make sure it won't catch fire.

Yes, of course a candle in a half coconut shell would be super cute, and can you imagine how many people would buy it? It would be great in tiki bars, at themed parties, for outdoor events – but it will also catch fire. So will soft plastic containers, bowls made out of wood or bark, and a whole host of other things.

If you have to question whether this item can literally catch fire, put it down and consider another route.

2. Make sure it won't crack.

Okay, this one is a little tricky – because it's kind of hard to know without testing the products. Do you remember a few years ago when gel candles were crazy popular, and there was a rumor going around they could explode? It wasn't actually the candles themselves exploding; it was candle makers choosing poor vessels for their candles. The fishbowl, or martini glass, or cheaply made glass shoe would crack under the heat, and glass and wax would go everywhere.

This is a big danger. Candle wax leaking everywhere will not only damage your customer's furniture or flooring, but it also presents a serious fire hazard (after all, wax is fuel). A wick with no wax pool will grow almost immediately, and could catch drapes, wood, and furniture on fire quickly.

Testing is going to be your best friend here, but also use common sense. Cheap glasses that you get from a thrift store or a dollar store probably can't withstand the heat of a candle. If it's not marketed as a candle holder, it probably shouldn't be one.

3. Make sure it won't leak.

Leaking wax is a big deal. Wax is hot, and a pain to clean, and if it leaks on the wrong thing it can do a lot of damage. If the amount of wax in a candle decreases too rapidly, the flame on the wick is going to grow too rapidly. This isn't what you want at all, and it could start a fire within just a few minutes.

Things leak that you might not expect, too, like a poorly-sealed metal container. Anything with a seam line has the potential to leak. I encourage you to test all of your containers by pouring water into the empty vessel and letting it sit for a few days. If you get water dripping, even slowly, from anywhere, know the candle container isn't suitable.

## Okay, so what can I use?!

Purchasing containers from wholesalers that are specifically made for candles is your best first step. They have taken all the guesswork out of whether these can be used to burn because, well, they have been extensively tested and proven to be safe.

High quality, relatively thick glass and flame-resistant materials are going to be your best bet. Remember, the container has to be able to withstand the heat of the wick and the melted wax.

In addition to glass, properly treated flower pots, ceramic bowls, and metal tins that are properly sealed are great choices. Again, be careful with anything that has a seam – but there are plenty of quality tins out there that will work perfectly.

Think not just of the material, but also the shape. If it is very wide on top and very narrow on the bottom, the heat is going to become more intense at the bottom; and the lower the wax level goes, the more dangerous it becomes. Think about the candles you see on the market – they are all relatively uniform in size, when it comes to a container. This is for a reason.

**It's okay to be creative. Just be safe.**

I know, you probably feel like I burst your bubble. You had all these ideas for a fun container or something unique, and now I've just rained on your parade. I'm sorry, but it's better you hear it from me than an angry customer whose candle leaked wax everywhere, ruining a very expensive piece of furniture.

You're totally allowed to be creative and unique, but make sure you do it within the confines of safety regulations. Otherwise, you're opening yourself up for a load of trouble, and putting your customers in an unsafe position.

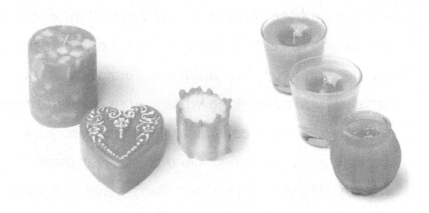

## How Testing Works

It is so important that you test your products extensively before you sell them. You wouldn't sell a cake from a recipe you've never tried before, after all. Candles shouldn't be any different. I touched on this briefly when I talked about ordering supplies, but let's go into it a little deeper.

Take your newly made (and ready to burn) candles, and set them on a heat-resistant surface. If you want to test multiple candles, make sure you clearly label which candle is which. This is a long process, so don't leave yourself any room for error. Any candles that are being tested should be at least 3 inches apart.

Make sure your wicks are an appropriate length – about a quarter of an inch – and then light each candle you're testing. Record the time you lit the candle, and keep the candles in your view at all times. If you're working while you're testing, make sure the testing area is clearly visible from your working area. You don't need to stare at them intently this entire time, but don't leave the room. That way, if a flame starts to get out of hand, you are right there to extinguish it.

After two hours, record the details of your candle. How big is the wax pool? How is the wick holding up? You should know by this point if there is something wrong with the wick or the wax – ideally, your candle will be burning evenly, not tunneling into the wax. The best candles will melt the wax to the edges of the container, leaving no waste.

After 4 hours, record the wax pool and wick condition again, and then blow out the candle. You should check the depth to make sure it's on track and study the candle. Is the wick mushrooming? Is the candle sooting? Is the pool significant? These could all be signs that your wick is too big.

Touch the container. Is it too hot? Is there leaked wax under it? What is the condition of the container?

Record all of your findings, and then let the candle cool for at least 5 hours. Then, repeat all of your steps until the candle is completely finished, taking care to log everything, including burn time. You can't just do this once – as the amount of wax is reduced, the burn quality is going to change.

If you get a final result that you're happy with, awesome! You've got a good set of candles. If your wax tunneled, leaked, or burned strangely; or if there was a lot of soot; or the container got dangerously hot, it's time to go back to the drawing board and figure out what went wrong.

Don't get upset if your first try isn't perfect. Heck, don't get upset if your third try isn't perfect. There is a lot of trial and error, and you're never going to nail it on the first pass all the time. Be patient with yourself and your blooming business. Proper testing is worth it. Not only for your peace of mind and a quality product, but for the satisfaction and safety of your customers.

# CHAPTER 9: WHAT'S IN A LABEL? WHAT'S IN A BOX?

When you're getting ready to ship your candles, there are a few important things you should be thinking of. Your packaging, and your label, for instance. Your very first in-person impression comes from the box you choose to ship, and your customer is going to get an impression of you from the labeling alone before they ever light your candle.

Making sure you spend time to get the best boxes and best labels for your target market, that line up with your brand, is going to make a big difference. Maybe not with the initial order, but you want repeat orders. It's important to remember that you're not just selling one candle once. Someone who buys today and loves it will come back and buy again, and recommend you to others, too. So make a good first impression and start off your relationship on the right foot.

## What's on Your Labels

Labels are tricky. They are one of the most direct ways you can communicate with your consumers, and you need to think long and hard about what you put on your candles.

First of all, you need your safety information – duh. We just talked about that. That should be a huge priority for you. After you have that taken care of, let's talk about what else should be on your label.

Your logo and company name should be easy to find, along with contact information – most commonly, a website. This lets your customers know immediately when they look at your product who made it and how to get more. It's the best and easiest way to get who you are across.

Any features or information about the product should be on there, too. Burn time, type of wax, and wick maintenance/trimming should all be included.

What scent the candle is, or what line it is from, should also be easy to find. Don't make your customers guess about what they are about to burn, especially if they purchased several different types of candles.

Wait, does this mean each type of candle needs a specific label?

Yes! Each product should have its own label. It's so important, and it really gives you a more professional, put-together look. Don't neglect it; once you've made one, it's not that difficult to make more.

If you're unsure how to label your products, take a look at the competitors, both in big box stores and online. Look at options you like and don't like. Can you easily see all of the important information? Can you tell what brand it is just by glancing at it? Does it appeal to their target market?

If you're struggling to design proper labels, you can hire a graphic designer to help you. Just like with every other instance of hiring someone, you will get better results when you know immediately what you want out of the situation. Go in with your logo, your branding information, and all of the most important info you want on the labels. The better prepared you are, the better the final product will be.

*Do I need a UPC code? What IS a UPC code?*

For most new candle-makers, the answer is no; you probably don't need a UPC code – but, depending on special factors, you might.

If you're planning on selling your candles locally only, not globally, you don't need a UPC code.

If you think you may ship internationally, then yes, you'll need a UPC code. When something is sold across the world, it has a standardization from one area to the other. The UPC code is basically that standardization, a unique number that is shown by a box of black lines which can be scanned.

Good news: it's not hard to do. You need to apply for a GS1 Company Prefix, which is going to be the first part of the UPC code. It's basically saying 'this is the company that made this product.' You can apply for a membership and license your prefix from GS1 directly.

Once you have gotten that, you can get assigned a unique product number. Each item that you sell will need a different product number, and that number is unique to that type of product.

Got that all settled? Then, figure out how you want to display the UPC on your products. Then, you can order your UPC barcodes and put them on your products to ship out.

If you're not going to ship internationally, you don't need to take this step. But registering and getting a UPC does open you up to being able to sell overseas, and it doesn't hurt at all.

## What Goes into a Box?

Once you've got your labels squared away, you need to think about the box that you're going to package and send your candles in.

Yes, you can go with just a generic box, and that's okay – especially at first. But if you want to level up your business, consider having custom boxes and shipping materials. This makes you look more professional, and less like someone working out of their basement. (Even if you are, in fact, working out of your basement!)

If you can't afford to have custom boxes printed, then consider using a large sticker of your logo that is designed for use on the boxes, or a stamp of your logo to put on the tissue paper. This takes extra time and a small amount of financial cost, but it lends professionalism to your overall product.

When you think about your ideal box and packaging, it should have your logo and your brand clearly visible to read. It should connect with your target market, and it should fit into your branding. It should also look like a natural extension of the product itself – the candle your customers pull out if it should seem to come from the same place.

*Note:* I know I've talked a lot about your target market up until this point. Don't worry; we're almost at the point of figuring out just who your target market is. It's coming!

Your contact information should also be clearly visible and easy to read. Whatever packaging material you have inside should be branded with your logo and your brand. Unpacking your products should be a fun, exciting experience for your customers. Think about how many 'unboxing' videos are on YouTube, after all!

As I said previously, this is an extra cost. If you can't swing it at first while you're dealing with startup costs, that is totally understandable. However, as you continue to grow, you should consider including these extra touches. It's one way you can stand out from the crowd, and offer a premium product.

If you're only shipping container candles, only a small amount of packaging material is probably going to be needed, especially depending on what container you're using. Be sure your boxes are not too big for your product (not just from a price standpoint, but a waste standpoint, too), and there is an appropriate cushion or filler to prevent breakage.

When shipping votive candles or pillar candles, make sure there is plenty of packaging. These candles may be your pride and joy, but USPS or UPS don't really care about that, and damage can easily happen in shipping. "Fragile" labels are a good investment, but most shipping companies don't really pay attention to that. However, it will give your customers a better, more secure feeling, which is worth it.

## Most Important: Be Honest

I cannot stress this enough: nothing on your packaging, either your labels, your information inside, or your shipping boxes, can be false. Do not put false claims of any nature on your products, and not just because it's questionable business practices to lie to your customers.

A group called the ASTM regulates the standards in a huge number of industries, including candle making. The National Candle Association, or NCA, has partnered with the ASTM to make candle standards across the board. Improper packaging and untruthful labeling are very much against standards, and it can get you in trouble.

It's also just a bad thing to do. Don't lie to your customers and tell them your candles burn for 50 hours when they burn for 20. Don't say it is 100%

soy when it's a paraffin/soy blend. This isn't how you keep customers, and it isn't good business practice.

The ASTM is a very valuable tool. Check out their standards for candle making, and be sure you understand them closely. This is going to save you time, hassle, and stress – and give you a better final product.

# CHAPTER 10: BUSINESS BASICS & STRATEGY

Alright, are you feeling good? By this point, the easiest (yikes, I know) part of the business is done. You've got the basics of making candles down. You understand the types of wax, the types of wicks, how to pour your candles, and more.

Now, we're going to talk about the harder stuff – the actual business side of things.

Note: There's a good chance you only skimmed the info before this. That's totally fine! If you had your process down already, or you felt confident in your candle making, you don't necessarily need to read anything before this. I do encourage you to do so, however. You can never have too much information about the product side of your business, and being confident in the technical aspect is so important. But, if you're jumping in here after the introduction, be sure you know your product, how to put it together, and how to present it.

Let's talk business strategy, shall we?

## The Basics of Business

At the very core of any business is an exchange of goods for money. You are going to give someone something – in this case, a candle – and in exchange, they are going to give you money. This is the core of every business, but there are thousands of other factors that can play a big part.

The biggest thing I can tell you is that the time you put into your business will pay off. You're going to understand this in the next few chapters, but passion or drive alone isn't going to make it, and a ton of time is going to go into your small business. If you only love making candles but you hate the idea of spending time dealing with customers, working on social media, marketing your business or working on a business plan – then running a business might not be for you. That's okay! Not everyone is cut out to own their own business, so don't feel bad.

Behind every successful small business is a handful of people (sometimes just one) working tirelessly. Spending nights or weekends, if they have another job. Getting up and grinding every single day to make their dream a reality. If you're not willing to put the time in to make your business successful, well, I'm not sure what to tell you – some of this is going to be hard.

But is it worth it? Absolutely, unquestionably. Being your own business, doing what you love, and making a great product feels amazing. If you have the desire and the drive, it is worth the time putting in. And I think, if you're reading this, you have that desire and that drive.

## What's a Business Plan, and Do You Need One?

Wait, where are you going? Are you skimming? Is your brain tuning out?

I understand; the technical side of things can be intimidating for a lot of people. Don't fret! I'm going to break all of this down in a way you can absolutely understand, even without a business or marketing degree. The words "business plan" might conjure up an image of boring men in suits sitting around a big conference table using buzzwords, but it doesn't have to be that way.

The best way I can describe a business plan is that it's your road map and your compass, all rolled into one. The business plan is going to tell you where you are, where you're going, and what your goal is. It will keep you motivated when you're feeling down or lost, and help you stay focused and end up with a successful business that makes you money and brings you joy.

Yes, you can make money and enjoy doing it! But first you need a plan.

## Before You Start

I highly recommend you read this with a notebook and a pencil in your hand. Take notes, answer my questions as you read along, and start thinking about how this applies to your business and your future. Then, come back to your notes and flesh out your business plan. You can also use a Word document if you'd rather type, or even make voice notes on your phone to transcribe later. Whatever works best for you.

## What's The First Element to a Successful Business Plan?

The very first element to creating a successful business plan is to consider your goals. This, I would argue, is probably the most important. Honestly, each step is going to be incredibly important to your final success (that I know you can achieve!).

You need to ask yourself if you want this candle-making business to be a lucrative, full-time operation or simply a side-hustle that generates some extra income and gives you a little bit of freedom.

There is no wrong answer, and I'm not going to shame you for whichever you choose. If you want a candle empire that will rival even the biggest brands, that's awesome! Dream big; you've got this! If you just want to spend a few hours a week pouring candles and making vacation money, that is awesome, too! There is nothing wrong with the old 5-9 grind that gives you some financial freedom.

It's okay to go a little crazy right now, but you have to realize that not everyone who sets out to start a candle-making empire makes it – and the chances of being a globally recognized candle-making king or queen are small. So while you can dream big, let's break down your business goals into realistic, bite-sized chunks so that, in a year or two, you're not discouraged if your candle-making empire isn't selling out in Europe or the Bahamas.

### Be specific and realistic.

Take a moment and think about realistic goals you have for the future that can be reasonably achieved. Write them down. Don't write I want to create extra income for my bottom line. Instead, write I want to earn at least $1,000 a month in net profit by the end of the year. One is vague and unhelpful; the other is direct and clear. I'm going to give you a tool to help you.

## Use SMART Goals

Have you heard of SMART goals? SMART is an acronym, and it's used in a lot of business classes to help you set and achieve your goals. It seems a little buzz-word-y, I know, but trust me, a SMART goal is good. It stands for:

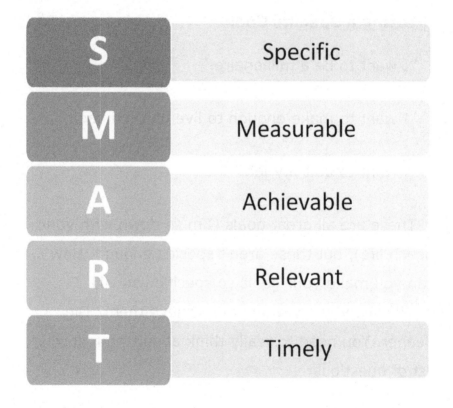

| S | Specific |
| M | Measurable |
| A | Achievable |
| R | Relevant |
| T | Timely |

Each goal you make for your business should be SMART. It should be specific, not vague. Measurable, not flexible. Achievable, not unrealistic. Relevant, not something completely out of left field. And timely, meaning that you have a set date – six weeks, six months, next year, whenever is realistic and achievable.

Does this make sense? Okay, let's break it down further.

## Creating a Specific Goal

"I want to be a millionaire."

"I want to make enough to live on the beach."

"I want to quit my job."

These are all great goals (I'm so down with your beach life), but these aren't specific enough. How can you make your goals so specific you will immediately know when you achieve them? Dig deeper. You need to really think about the following list of questions:

- What is it that you want to accomplish?

- What do you wish to make happen?

- Where can you make this goal a reality?

- Who is going to be involved in the success of your goal?

- Why is this goal important to you?

For every goal you set, ask yourself these questions, and write down the answers in bullet-point form. If you can't answer these questions for each goal you're setting yourself, then your goal is not specific enough. Dig deeper.

## Creating a Measurable Goal

This one is a little easier to achieve than your 'specific' goal, but it is so important that hitting your goals is measurable and realistic. If you can't measure your goals, how do you know when you've hit one?

With each goal, ask yourself – how much? How many? How and when will I know this goal is accomplished, and I've succeeded? Once you know the very specifics of your goal like this, you know it's measurable. If you can't answer these questions, go back to the drawing board and take another look at your goals.

## Creating an Achievable Goal

Becoming a millionaire from candle making is a great goal, but that isn't an achievable goal at the start. Don't get me wrong, I'm not doubting your ability to get there eventually! But maybe hit a more immediately achievable goal, first. For example:

"Ship 100 candles by x date", or "Streamline the system to allow the creation of x and y number of candles per hour/day." These are good, measurable, possible goals.

On the other hand, "Become nationally recognized," "Ship millions of candles," or "Be inspiring" aren't great goals. You can't measure them, and you probably can't attain them—at least not the first two.

## Creating a Relevant Goal

Is this goal appropriate, realistic, and in line with who you are and what you can accomplish? Does it meet a need for/speak to your customers?

Think about your target market and the world at large. What is relevant to that? Extreme, rapid expansion might not be relevant or possible within a down economy or in a tough area. Expanding your business and moving into a new workshop within the year might not be a relevant goal when you've got plenty of space right now, and need that money to go to other things.

A relevant goal is worthwhile, matches/supports your other goals, and most of all, matches you and your business. Your goals should always be relevant not only to you, and your business, but as a whole.

## Creating a Timely Goal

Timely, or time-based, goals are so important! When there is no time frame attached to your goal, there is no urgency or concern. Set dates and times you wish to complete your goals, and follow through to the best of your abilities.

"Ship x number of candles" is a fine goal, but with no time limit, it falls flat. Instead, "ship x amount of candles by y date" is more focused and specific.

When looking at timeframes, consider: When will it be done? What can I do today, tomorrow, and this week? What can be done in six weeks? What do I need to accomplish by the end of this quarter/this year?

The more specific you are, the better. Be realistic and hold yourself to your own standards.

## Now, Put It All Together

What do you have? SMART goals! Each goal that you lay out for your business needs to go through the SMART goal frame of reference. If even one of your goals fails one of these questions, go back to the drawing board and be more specific.

SMART goals are also great in your personal life, but I'm not here to tell you how to run your own life – just to help you run your business!

Do you think this is too many steps? It's too complicated/too much hassle/too tedious? I can understand where you're coming from, but remember that so many major business leaders and business classes use this exact process. I didn't just make this up for you. All of these people couldn't be wrong.

As long as all of your goals help define and push your business forward, and they are SMART goals, you are on the path to success.

## Who is Your Target Market, and Why?

Here's something to think about – who is your target market, and why are they your target? Are you selling to middle-aged mothers working part-time with kids in school? On-the-go professionals trying to get some relaxation in at night? Older empty nesters looking to re-invent their home now that they don't have kids?

The answer "everyone!" seems like a good answer at first, because there are billions of people in this world. The more people you can target, the more your sales are – right? Well, no. If your market is too broad, and you become generic, trying to make everyone happy, you end up appealing to no one at all. As a small, growing business, the only way you can truly compete with 'the big guys' is to target a niche market. The narrower, at least to start, the better.

Think about it this way: It's a lot better to focus your target on 1,000 people that are perfect for your product, than 10,000 or even 100,000 who couldn't care less.

Let's take some time, now that you've got some goals aligned, to talk about your target market and who you're selling to. Here are some questions to help you narrow your focus:

- What is the age range of your ideal buyer?

- What does your ideal buyer do for an income?

- What does your ideal buyer like to do in their time off work?

- What education does your ideal buyer have?

- Where does your ideal buyer live? In the US, outside of the US?

- Is your ideal buyer married? Single? Engaged?

- Where is your ideal buyer from?

Think about your product line while you're answering these questions, and form a picture of the perfect buyer. Maybe it's a late 20's mother-of-one with minimal higher education who lives in the South and has a small budget each month for home décor and self-care.

Maybe your buyer is a 30-something child-free professional pulling in 5 figures on her own who likes to treat herself to a nicer version of things living in a big city on the East Coast.

Maybe... Okay, you get the point, right?

Spend some time figuring out your target market. Your product is going to drive your target market. If you're creating candles that smell like cookies and candy, your target market probably isn't 60-something retired men who like to travel. If your scents are primarily leather, pine, woods, and rain, a 19-year-old college student studying fashion design who enjoys romance movies and dreams of her wedding might not be interested in what you have to sell.

When you've figured out who you would love to sell to, think about whether your choice is a good one. Ask yourself:

- Does this make sense?

- Are there enough people in my target market to realistically sell to?

- Do these people have a need for my product? Can they afford my product?

- How can I easily reach these people with my product?

- What market is currently overlooked by other products/brands that I can target?

I personally find, at least at first, to choose a target market that you have common ground with. Whether you're both moms, from a similar area/background, same age group – whatever it is. You're going to find crafting products and marketing a lot easier if you connect with your ideal buyer.

If you only have 50 people in your target market, maybe you've gone a little too deep. Try to find a balance between a healthy market that you can sell to and access easily, and a market that is specific enough to need your product.

## Why Your Target Market Matters

Defining your target market isn't just about getting a better idea of who you're selling to. It's also about saving money. This may be one of the most important things you define, and it's going to set the tone for your whole business, your marketing strategy, everything moving forward.

You're going to pay for marketing eventually. Maybe not immediately, but there will come a time sooner or later that you want to expand your business and sell more. So, you're going to look at other marketing tools – promoted posts on social media, ads, in-person sales, etc.

You could spend a ton of money throwing a huge net and hoping to collect a few customers. Alternatively, you could spend a smaller amount of money targeting your users where you know they frequent – Pinterest, Instagram, a podcast's advertisement space, etc – and get a lot more bang for your buck. Again, even if you're technically reaching fewer people, it's all about quality, not quantity.

Your target market is so important. Skipping this step when forming your business is asking for disaster later – and a whole lot of wasted money.

## Find What's Missing

Sometimes called positioning in the business world, you should work on being intimately familiar with your direct competitors, and figure out what they're missing that you can supply.

Maybe your groove will be offering unique scents that are a little off the wall. Perhaps it's creating a solid line of natural soy candles in bright, light scents.

Maybe your competitors are really missing tealight candles, or giant candles that last for 40+ hours with multiple wicks, or candles slightly bigger than a tea light for samples/scent testing purposes.

You get the gist.

Look at scents, styles, and sizes, as well as marketing. Find what is missing, and think about how you can fill the gap.

# The Most Awkward Topic: Money and Pricing

Yes, we're still talking about your business plan! There's a lot that goes into this, and it's incredibly important at each step, so be patient. I know this isn't the fun part of running a business, but getting your foundation good is essential to your success.

Pricing is a really difficult thing for a beginner to think about, and it's easy to want to marginalize your time to cut your competitors. Finding your best price point also can be complicated, so it's totally understandable if you're feeling overwhelmed thinking about everything that goes into pricing your products.

I'm going to do my best to break down pricing in an easy-to-follow way, but ultimately I can't tell you the pricing that is right for you.

You need to take a hard look at your costs, your time, and assign a fair number. All the sales in the world aren't going to make your business succeed if you're not charging enough, and ultimately losing money on the business.

## What to Consider When Pricing

When calculating the price of your candles, take into account the cost of raw materials, fixed costs, overhead, packaging, and marketing, at a minimum. Each time you sell a candle, you need to recoup the costs of making and sending that candle – the total costs above. And please, do not forget to calculate a decent hourly wage for yourself in this, too. I'm certainly not suggesting you make $100/hour, but it is not sustainable to not pay yourself during this process!

Okay, for a very simple breakdown of figuring out your cost, use this (very, very basic) formula:

### *Unit cost = cost of batch / total number of units*

If your batch of 100 small candles costs you $200 to make, package, and prepare, your unit cost is $2. You can't sell your candles for that $2 price tag, though!

That is your unit cost. Your selling price needs to be higher, in order to bring in profit and keep yourself, and the business, successful. If your unit cost is $2, and you're selling for $5, that is a profit of $3 per candle. Sound obvious? Okay, good – but like I've said a thousand times, your foundation is so important!

If you take a business class, there are three 'main' ways to set prices that benefit both you and the consumer. Maybe you know these – maybe you took a business class in college. But if you're like most people and you're learning as you read this guide, these principles can help.

**1. The Fixed Price Strategy** is the simplest pricing model you'll ever find, and the simplicity makes it very attractive to most new business owners. If you have a fixed amount of income you want to make each month, or year, look at your products and add that amount to the cost of your candles. If you're selling 500 candles a month, and you want to make at least $1,000 in profit each month, you need to make sure you're adding $2 to your fixed cost.

The fixed price strategy has some benefits – it's very easy to understand, and very straightforward – but it is limiting. This strategy can be great for new business owners, but isn't necessarily sustainable as you grow.

**2. The Multiplier Strategy** takes some math, but it is appealing in the way that you will always make a set amount of profit no matter what your product is. When you are calculating your final price, you look at the unit cost and multiply – hence the name. If you want to sell your product at 2x what it cost you, and your candle cost $2 to make, you'll sell it for $4. If it costs $10 to make, and you want to sell your products at 1.5x the cost, you'll charge $15.

**3. The Percentage Strategy.** This is similar to the multiplier strategy above. If you want to use a percentage instead of a set number, this is for you. If you want to sell your candles for 50% more than you made, figure out what 50% of your unit cost is, and add that on. If your unit cost of a candle is $2, your selling price will be $3. If your unit cost is $10 and you want to sell your candles for 65% more, you'll be selling your candle for $16.50. Make sense?

When you're figuring out what strategy you're going to go with, and your price points for your candles, be sure to take into account – you guessed it – your target market. If you're marketing yourself for early-20's moms, their budget for fancy candles won't be the same as 50-something professionals.

If you're looking at wholesale prices, this is an entirely different conversation. You need to make your wholesale prices attractive, so that you're making money and the re-seller is making money. Pricing should always be above the lowest profitable price, but not as high as you're reselling it for yourself.

There's a good chance you won't be working with resellers and making wholesale prices at first, but this all depends on your market and your goals.

If you aren't doing wholesaling right away, don't worry about this pricing for now – once you get your process down and start making money, it will be easier for you to figure out how much it will be worth to you to wholesale your product.

## What Are Financial Projections?

Financial projections are a little bit of a step up when you're looking at numbers and finances, and if you consider yourself someone who is bad at numbers, this might be intimidating. There are a lot of benefits to having good financial projections, and they provide you a level of security since you will know what is coming.

Financial projections help in a few different ways, especially at first. They will help you understand your startup costs and forecast future sales. Both of these things are very important!

## What Does Forecasting Sales Mean?

Literally every successful business in existence uses financial projections to forecast sales and predict future sales. When you know your target market, your profit margins, and past sales, you can realistically calculate your revenue in the coming weeks and months (barring any major changes).

Making a financial projection means calculating the number of units you will realistically sell in the coming months and your profit. First, consider what you have sold in the previous months, then allow for your projected growth (if you sold 2% more candles each month for the past 12 months, you can bet you'll sell at least 2% more each month going forward), and take into account any marketing you're doing. Multiply your realistic number of units by the selling price of each unit.

If you project, based on past sales, that you will sell 500 candles next month at a selling price of $12/candle, you can project $6,000 in sales.

When you first start your business, much of this is unknown, so forecasting isn't going to be incredibly helpful. But as you grow and expand, and gain a following, this is going to be absolutely vital.

Don't hesitate to ask other vendors that you're close with what their projected sales are, how much they are selling of an item in a month or a year, and see what the 'industry standard' looks like.

Something to keep in mind: A mass-market 6-oz candle sells for between $5-$8, roughly. A mid-market candle, between $9 and $14. A high-end market candle of that size is about $15-$22. People pay for quality when it comes to candles!

Depending on your target market, you'll probably fit into one of these three ranges. Think a lot about who you're selling to, what they can afford, and the final product you want to put out.

## Projecting Startup Costs

Financial projections also can help with your startup costs, and this is incredibly important for a young business. So many people underestimate their startup costs, and fail before they ever get started.

Make sure you are brutally honest when calculating your startup costs, and leave yourself plenty of wiggle room for unexpected expenses.

Here's an idea of what your list should look like. These aren't actual figures, just an idea of what your own list of startup costs should look like.

Base Ingredient Cost: $300
Equipment Cost: $300
Packaging, Labeling, Shipping: $300
Permits and Registration: $1,000

Marketing: $500

Insurance: $400

Cushion Room/Extras: $300

Total: $3,100

Overhead Costs: Approximately 15% of previous costs, or $465

**Real life total: $3,565**

This is a good base calculation. Your expenses might be different – you may have a high monthly rent price (not recommended, but we've talked about this). Maybe you need very little equipment because you already own much of it. Perhaps you don't need a ton of marketing right away because you have a strong base audience.

I recommend making two startup cost estimations, one conservative estimation and one aggressive estimation. What is the worst-case scenario for costs that you can think of? What is the best case? Record both, and you'll have a good idea of the spectrum.

Finally, we have the last piece of your business plan. The one no one really wants to think about, but always should.

## What's Your Exit Plan?

You will always want to have an exit plan, or exit strategy, on standby. It doesn't matter if you want to keep this as a side job a few hours a week to make vacation money, or you want to grow this to be a full-time gig that blossoms into a huge company.

An exit plan helps you prepare for the worst-case situation before it ever becomes a situation. It allows you to be ready to handle anything, and you never have to have any panic in the back of your mind as to what you should do if something terrible happens.

Think long and hard about what you want your ideal exit strategy to be.

Handing the business off to a trusted friend or family member happens more than you'd think. You can stay involved in the business without being too invested, and you're giving your "candle baby" to someone you trust. This is a great option if you have friends or family you trust that are interested, but know that it can breed resentment, and you could be opening yourself up for conflict or issues.

Another option is to sell your business. As you gain success, you may even run into offers from other businesses who want to absorb what you're doing into their process. This comes with risks, and it's important to remember that the more profit you make, the more your business will sell for, either from an investor or on the open market. If you're looking to abandon a sinking ship, this isn't the best choice.

Liquidation is the most common option for a business that has failed. You're going to get the lowest return on investment, but it's also the easiest. Anything you've purchased for the business – space, equipment, supplies – are all assets. When you sell these off, either one at a time or altogether, you're liquidating your assets. This is one way to get at least some of the money you've invested back.

## Putting It All Together

A successful **Business Plan** truly has six components. Now that you've thought about your target market, your questions, and your goals, let's dive into these real quick.

1. **An Executive Summary** is the first step, and it's an overview of what your business is and what your plans are for the business.

2. **Opportunity** is an important section in your business plan, and it's basically answering the questions we have talked about previously – what are you selling? What is the problem that you're solving? Who is your competition? What is your target market, and why?

3. The **Execution** section is going to talk about how you are going to make this a reality. How will you execute your plans to keep your business running successfully? How can you utilize the opportunity to be successful?

4. A **Company Summary** is basically all of the reasons that someone should invest in your business. Even if you don't plan on having investors, this is an important section. Go on to describe the type of people you plan on hiring, too – even if you're not hiring right now, looking to the future is important. Providing the history of your business and your passion is also good in this section.

5. Your **Financial Plans** are also important, and will help you stay on track moving forward. This is something that you'll continue adding to – at

first, it might be bare. Cost analysis, pricing, sales forecasts (we'll talk all about this in a moment, hang tight), and more should go in here. Anything financially important should be in this section.

6. Finally, an **Appendix** should close out your business plan. Product images, important business information, and anything else that an investor might want to know but doesn't fit in any other segment should be added here.

I know this sounds like a lot to put together, and in a way, it is. This is very intimidating for a new business owner, but I don't recommend putting your business plan off. Having clear goals, guidelines, and projections is going to help you become successful in the future, and you'll feel more like a real business. After all, you're running a business now.

## Does This All Make Sense?

These are the basic building blocks of a good business plan. Now you, as a business owner, need to put all these pieces together to create a cohesive plan that fits your market, your goals, and your own business.

I encourage you to take your time with this process. Start it, step away, think on it some, and come back to it. As your business grows and you find success, your goals will be achieved – and new ones will be added. Continue to follow these rules, and you'll be set up for success in no time.

# CHAPTER 11: MARKETING, PART ONE

Marketing is so important. I cannot stress it enough, good marketing will make a terrible company popular, and bad/nonexistent marketing will make an incredible product never hit the market or sell.

This can be so overwhelming for new businesses and new business owners, because most of us don't have a degree in marketing. But you don't need to be an expert, or know all the lingo, to handle marketing for your business.

At some point down the line, you can hire a professional to handle your marketing. But if you're going in this with the lowest costs possible and starting out on your own, or with just the help of friends and family, you're probably going to have to tackle marketing yourself.

I'm going to break this up into a few different segments so you can really get a good idea of how to approach marketing and growing your business. You don't have to read it all right now, but I encourage you to do so, and continue to take notes in your notebook. As your business grows and you get deeper into the marketing, revisit these sections and see how you can improve what you're doing or change it up.

## Let's Talk Branding

Branding is so very important. I know, I know; I just said marketing was important – but a huge part of your marketing process is going to be branding, especially early on. Think of your brand as your identity, a core part of your business. Every single decision you make, be it packaging, scents, or marketing, should be driven by your brand.

Make sure you take into consideration your target market before you settle on brand identity or back story. It should be in line with who you're selling to, and why. If your target market can't connect with your brand, they have no incentive to purchase your products or support you.

Distance yourself from negativity, discrimination, or anything, well, bad. This seems obvious, but it's easy to get caught up in 'cancel culture' or to push the envelope to try and be funny or cute to set yourself apart. You're not doing yourself any favors, here – don't alienate a big portion of your target market by being "too much".

Are you a little confused? Branding is much more than a logo or a design. It's a message you send to your consumers, and it's so important to be able to convey that in a clear way. Take a fresh piece of paper in your notebook, think about these questions I'm about to ask, and start writing down words or phrases that line up with your own core values, or the values of your company. It doesn't have to be a cohesive sentence or paragraph yet. Think of it as a word cloud, with the most important ones large and bold.

**Who Are You?** Who are you, the owner? Who are you, the brand? You're not dumping millions of dollars into start-up costs (I assume), so you shouldn't come across as another faceless corporation. Make it clear to your consumers that you are a person who cares about their life, their job, their business, the community, the environment – whatever. Your own nature should shine through.

**What Do You Do?** What product do you have to sell? What are you making to give to people? Many brands choose to present a "problem" to the reader and offer the solution they created, effectively being the hero in their own story. Remember the story I told you at the beginning of the book, the reason I got into candle making? I was having headaches and issues with fragrances, and creating my own candles fixed that. That's a real story, but it's also a great branding moment.

**Who Do You Do It for?** Who is your target market? Who do you want to reach? Who are you trying to help or support with your business?

**Why Do You Do It? Why Do You Care?** This is the section where you show people why you care. Why did you create your company? What drove you to candles, to your target market, to these products, and this branding? What solutions are you trying to create with this business?

**How Do You Do It? What's Your Process?** Okay, this is the fun section – the part where you talk about your process. Why did you choose your particular ingredients, how do you craft your candles, and why does it matter? Are safety and quality important? Talk about it!

**What's in the Future?** Where do you see yourself and your company in five years? Ten years? Talk about your short- or long-term goals for the company and how you can achieve them. This doesn't have to go as in-depth as your business plan, obviously, but touch on your future with the company. This shows consumers you aren't looking to up and leave; you're here to stay.

## Make It Personal

Your story should be personal. It should connect the readers to you; your consumers shouldn't just feel like they're buying candles from a random company, but a real person. This will immediately help you stand out from the crowd and separate you from the big-box options.

Your story should also be authentic. Even if it's not strictly 100% true, you should not go to a competitor's site and rip off their core values or ideas. It's totally fine to compare notes, but creating an authentic story is important.

Don't be afraid to be emotional in your story and your brand. Humans constantly crave an emotional connection, and if they can get that from your brand, that is even more incentive for them to purchase from you.

Finally, it's okay to boil it down to something simple. This doesn't have to be a 5-page intro about your whole life, because then you'll lose readers and customers. Make it simple, easy to digest, emotional, personal, and authentic; and you're going to have a winner.

## Your Brand Name & Logo

Okay, so you've got a story. It's personal, it's emotional, it answers all the important questions, and your customers know exactly who you are and why they should buy from you, right?

Think about your **company name.** You might already have a name in mind, or you may have already ordered packaging or business cards with that name. That's okay. But ask yourself: Does your name convey what it should? Does it fit in with your target market? What about your story and your branding? If the answer is no to any of these, or even a hesitant maybe, stop and reconsider it.

When it comes to the name of your product lines and your scents, you should be asking the same questions. Does it fit with your branding? Is it easy to say and easy to spell? Is it easy to remember, or catchy? Getting too wordy is going to turn off your customers, and using big, "smart" words or phrases might sound cool to you, but if your target market isn't going to appreciate it, you're just going to be losing people.

**Note**: Once you've settled on a name, *please please please* do your research to ensure that no one else has used that name. We're going to talk about how to check on this more in the legalities chapter, but you are responsible for making sure your name is unique.

If you have a line of scents or products, make sure no other competitor is using that name, or a similar name, for their own products. Do this research before you commit to it, because there is nothing worse than falling in love with a name, creating labels and designs, and as soon as you bring your product to market you realize someone has done this first.

Now you need a **logo**, a graphic or picture that goes with your name. When it comes to logos, think carefully about what you want to convey. If you don't have any experience with graphic design or art,

I highly recommend hiring out the logo process. There are countless freelance graphic designers available for a variety of price points, and even a cheap choice is a good investment. Check out sites like **Fiverr.com**, where you can find graphic designers for a very low cost (like, $5) to do logo design, business and stationary, flyers and brochures, and overall brand style.

No matter if you decide to tackle your logo yourself or hire out, have a good idea of what you would ideally want it to look like or convey before you begin. Do you have a color scheme for your brand? Does it match what your target market likes? Do you want a big blocky font, or a curving script?

If you're hiring out, find a few logos that you really love to show as examples. Note what you like about the logos – the style, the minimalism, the colors, etc. This will help you get a final product you're really happy with, and make your designer's life a lot easier, too.

Once you have your brand name, logo, font, and style, be sure to look at them on a variety of devices to make sure they appear the way you want them to. In other words, don't just look at them on your computer. Look at them on your phone, on a laptop, on a tablet, on a friend's computer, print them out. Some things don't translate well across platforms, so you want yours always looking the best.

## Do I Need a Website?

Website creation is probably the biggest intimidator for new business owners. I get it! Coding is scary, and you might be thinking of the days that you needed to be a whiz to create your own website. Nowadays, it's a lot simpler.

There are plenty of free website creation hubs where you can pay absolutely nothing to host your site, but these come with heavy negatives, too. This is your business, and you should be calculating these expenses in your startup and ongoing costs.

Your website shouldn't just be "good enough" – it should be good! If your site has a weird URL (many "free" sites force you to use their own extensions), looks poorly put together, or screams amateur, people will be less likely to purchase your products.

Would you give your credit card info or shipping information to a site that looked slapped together?

There are plenty of WordPress plugins or themes you can use that are easy to customize, and look great. Most of these are free, or at least very cheap. If you're still uncomfortable with creating your own website, you can also hire someone. Just like with a graphic designer, there are plenty of freelancers online who can make your website dream a reality.

Once again, just like with your designer, go into the project with a clear goal in mind. How many pages do you want on your site? What do you want it to be able to do? To look like? How should it function? The clearer idea you have in mind, the better the final project will be.

This can range in price from a hundred dollars to a thousand dollars. It's going to depend on who you hire, where you find them, and what you need. Don't go with the first person who offers to help, and make sure you shop around to find someone you connect with.

Once you have set up your website, it's important that you look at it from a *customer's* perspective. Is your information easy to find? Can you identify where everything is? Is it laid out in a way that is appealing and easy to use?

So many small businesses suffer from poor websites and poor navigation, and they scare their customers away before they ever make a purchase. Take the extra time to ensure that everything is easy to read and easy to find. I encourage you to ask close friends or a mentor to walk through the site, too, to ensure that it isn't painful, slow, or awkward to use. This is absolutely vital to a successful business.

What if you're planning to do most of your sales in person? Is a website really necessary? I cannot stress this enough: even if you're selling in-person, you need a website! You need marketing! You need branding! Also, your website should be easy to find on all your candles for reordering purposes. Plus, if someone gifts your candle, they can easily see where to buy more.

## Do I Need a Professional Photographer?

This is a hard question, and it's going to depend on a lot of things, but the answer is maybe. Do you have a good-quality camera? I'm not talking about your phone's camera, but an actual camera that will produce high-resolution shots.

You're going to want to stage each product in a way that is visually appealing and easy to identify. Don't hide it behind flowers or grass, even if it looks artsy. You don't want your customers to struggle to read your labels or see your products. Every bit of your site should be attractive, easy to navigate, and easy to read.

Think about where you can take these pictures. If you have a lovely room in your house with excellent lighting, this could be a great backdrop. A generic backdrop and good lighting – like a sturdy sheet and an overhead light – can work, too. Make sure you're honest with yourself about the results, however. Would this picture make you want to buy this product? If the answer is no, or not really, it's time to re-stage and re-shoot.

If you don't have a camera that can take these pictures, there are a few options for you. You could approach friends or family and see if they have a camera you could use for product photos.

If you don't have any other options, you should consider hiring a professional. It's not as expensive as you might think, depending on your area, and you won't need a ton of photos starting out. Local photography schools, or even colleges with an art department, might be able to refer you to a student for a relatively low price to help build their portfolio. Shop around.

Remember, when your customers are buying something online, all they have are your photos and your words to go by. Having clear, attractive pictures is going to be the difference between a sale and an abandoned cart – or no one ever clicking that button at all.

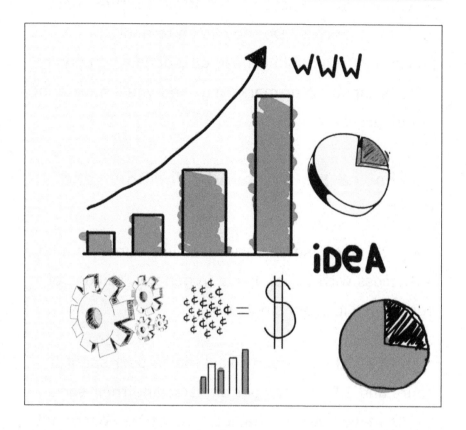

Advertising: the beast that so many people are scared of. If you haven't realized it yet, running a business is a lot more than just pouring candles and choosing wicks. Advertising your business can seem very intimidating; but just like anything else, it's not as hard as you think it is, I promise! And yes, once again, it's going to circle back to your target market.

Where does your target market spend their time? Is it Instagram? Facebook? Twitter? Do they follow lots of influencers? Do they listen to a lot of podcasts? Think about these questions when you're thinking about your marketing, and you'll have a lot more success.

## Facebook & Instagram Ads: The Down and Dirty

Hands down, small businesses like ours find a lot of success with social media in general. Millions of people use it every single day.

In 2020, the average social media user spent 2 hours and 24 minutes per day scrolling their social media feeds overall. That's a ton of time. We're not going to get into the psychology of spending that much time online, but know it's a great way to reach your audience.

Let's take a look at Facebook advertising for a moment, and talk about some best practices to help you set yourself up for success.

## Facebook ads

Facebook is one of the best ways for small businesses to advertise. First of all, it's crazy easy to use, which can be dangerous. New business owners have a tendency to blow a ton of cash on Facebook ads that aren't successful, and then get very discouraged. So it's best to take it step-by-step and see what the return is.

The basics are this: After creating your business page, make a post about a product, product line, or your new business in general. Hit the promote icon and set up an advertising campaign for as long as you'd like. You should be able to control your target audience, and Facebook will let you know your potential reach.

Set a budget for how much you want to spend on this campaign, and how long you would like it to run, and Facebook does the rest.

Sounds easy, right? It is. But there are a few things to keep in mind:

- Plan ahead: develop a strategy, choose an objective, and know your target audience. For example, are you trying to sell more of a certain soap, or promote a new product, or enlarge your email list? Think about what you are trying to accomplish with each ad post.

- Be sure to use a good, clear, interesting image in your ad post. Never do a text-only ad; people just don't pay any attention to them.

- If you can do a video, even better. Video posts generally engage even more people than photo posts. This isn't realistic for everyone, but if you have the ability to promote a video post, you should.

- Limit the frequency of your ad posts. Try one ad post per week or every two weeks to start off, and watch to see how it performs. Don't get carried away too quickly. You don't want to blow your advertising dollars on posting too frequently before you learn what works best.

- Keep track. Don't be afraid to do a/b testing with different versions of ad content, especially when you first start. Find out what type (see next point), tone, and phrasing works best with your target audience. Keep track of your advertising campaigns, and take note of what is most successful. Learn to use Facebook Ad Center (found by going to your page and clicking More). Keeping track doesn't have to be complicated – you can even use a Google Sheet or Doc with all the information from each ad every month.

- Experiment with different types of ads. For example, a "Like Ad" asks viewers to Like your page and connects them to your page for future promotions and communication. As you grow your page fans/followers, you will be able to post/advertise to them for free and form relationships with them simply through posting on your page. Look up other ad types like "sponsored stories" or "domain ads." (These ads take people off of Facebook and onto a web page, so you want to offer them a strong incentive to do so—like a discount or special offer.)

- Finally, mobile users are going to be your bread and butter. The vast majority of social media use comes from mobile devices, be it phones or tablets. And how often are you yourself guilty of this – opening social media to scroll on your phone while waiting in line, lying in bed, sitting on the couch watching commercials, etc.

## Your Facebook business page

The above section is about your Facebook ads; this section is about your main Facebook business page. There are certain things to keep in mind to make your Facebook page more appealing and useful. For example, the content or frequency of your posts. Learn what people respond to.

How do you do this? **Facebook Page Insights**. You'll want to find and monitor this page carefully. This will help you as you continue to post and grow to find a good rhythm and posting routine, and see what is working for you. To find the Facebook Page Insights, go to your Facebook page and click Insights in the top menu. If you don't see 'Insights,' click More. This takes you to your Overview (which you can also access by clicking Overview in the left-hand menu). Overview will give you an at-a-glance look at how your page is doing: page views, likes, post reach, etc.

*Limit the frequency* of your posts, as long as the relevancy is there. It's better to have one post per day or a few per week than multiple posts during the day. You don't want to blow up your target market's social media feed with your content – quality is better than quantity.

**Content:** Don't hard sell all the time. Yes, your end goal is sales – but providing helpful, funny, or informational content is going to go a long way to endear your brand. You are going to reach more people this way, and get better engagement overall, which is a huge win. Find a good balance in your posts.

**Easy to Use:** When you maintain your Facebook page, there are a few key things to keep in mind. First of all, go on the site as a user and try to find information. Is your business website easy to find? Your phone number? A description of your business or your products? Do you have all your content well organized? How much does a user have to sort through to find your product listings, relevant pictures, and more?

This is often overlooked, especially by first-time business owners, but it's so important. I can't tell you how many times I personally have gotten frustrated with a small business's Facebook page while trying to find information out about them and just given up. Instead, my business went elsewhere.

***Use Stories:*** With both Facebook and Instagram, make sure you are utilizing the Stories functions often. It's a more casual way of reaching your consumers, and it increases the likelihood of engagement. You don't even always have to post about your product – a funny story, a repost of something that matches your brand's values, or even a cute cat picture all work! At least one story a day should be posted, but don't be afraid to do 2-3 posts. Make sure you sprinkle in product placements or pictures, especially pictures from customers or testimonials, but again, avoid too much of the hard sell. You're playing the long game here.

Okay, let's talk about Instagram ads for a moment.

## Instagram ads

First of all, after you have a good presence on Facebook, you should definitely consider using Instagram for your business. Instagram is one of the top mobile apps downloaded, period. So many people use Instagram in many, many different ways. How you use it will depend on your target market and how they utilize the platform, but Instagram is a great tool.

Just like with Facebook, you should have a business Instagram page that promotes your brand and links back to your website. You cannot link to your store within your Instagram post, but you can use a Link in Bio tool – like Tap.Bio, Shorby, Lnk.Bio, or Linktree – to connect your posts to specific pages on your site.

Don't be afraid to link all your social media accounts together. Instagram, Facebook, and Twitter can all connect to one another, and this makes it easy to make a single post in multiple places.

Finally, just like with Facebook, make sure your business Instagram page aligns with your brand, too. Does it have the right branding? The right look? The right color? Is this something your target audience will immediately associate with your brand? If the answer is no, tweak it some more!

Hashtags are vitally important on Instagram, and if you're a regular Instagram user, you know this. Users can search for a specific hashtag, or click on a hashtag from another post to explore more. Be careful of overdoing it, though – some research suggests that the ideal number of hashtags is between 7 and 30, which seems a huge number, honestly. I suggest less than 20, but more than 4.

If you open up Instagram on your desktop and search for a hashtag, you will also get related hashtags – and how many posts they have.

For example, #candles have 14 million posts. #candlesofinstagram has over 820,000 posts. #candleshop has half a million. #soycandles has over 2 million. You get the point.

Variations of hashtags change the number of posts, too. #soywaxcandles has just over 630,000 posts, which is a lot but not as many as #soycandles. Yes, you can double-dip.

Using popular hashtags will increase the chances of someone organically finding your content, which is great. This is what you want, without a doubt. Be wary of using hashtags with only a few posts, as they won't be doing much for you. The only exception? If you want a brand hashtag.

If your business is, say, Luxury Candles by Lindsay, #CandlesbyLindsay or #LuxuryCandlesbyLindsay could be added to every post you make – and you can ask your customers to post photos of your products using that hashtag, too.

Don't be afraid to drop hashtags in the top comments, too. If you find your hashtags are cluttering up your post and making it hard to read, dropping those hashtags in the comments is a good alternative.

Paid ads on Instagram work very similarly to Facebook, in which you can target your specific market and increase your exposure. Only promote ads or posts that are well thought out, well-constructed, interesting, and engaging. Remember, while selling is the ultimate goal, building up a strong base is also very important.

## How Else Can I Utilize Facebook or Instagram?

It's not just about promoting your posts and pushing ads, though that is very important. Make sure you're checking your social media accounts daily to **form bonds** with your customers.

Facebook especially is great for handling **customer service** issues, as you can respond quickly from anywhere – a big deal in today's world where our customers expect instant communications. When you're just starting out, I advise you to encourage your customers to direct-message you on social media if they need something. This is going to be easier to maintain than an email account, for instance, and it will give your brand a sense of personality and personalization. This is something that really lacks with larger brands, and can absolutely set you apart.

You should also be **interacting** with your customers. If someone posts a comment on a picture or video, thank them. Like pages where your target audience hangs out, and comment. Don't hard sell on an unrelated post, but engaging people can go a long way to getting your brand noticed.

Don't be afraid to encourage **discussions** with questions, polls, or stories. Ask your customers what they value, what they want to see next, or even just questions about themselves. Show that you care about your customers, and that you value their opinions.

## Should I Use Influencers?

An influencer is a person on social media (Instagram specifically, but the term tends to overlap other social media) with a large following, who influences the people they follow. Influencers can be beauty gurus, home experts, fitness superstars, celebrities even. If they have a lot of followers and many people see their content, that's what matters.

So, should *you* use Influencers? This is a tricky question, because there is a lot of split information on the subject of using influencers. Some marketing gurus think using an influencer is absolutely the best way to grow your audience via social media, while others think it may damage or 'cheapen' your brand.

Personally, I think when used right, influencers can be great. But make sure you're always making your money back on what you spend.

Make sure when you're choosing an influencer that you're picking someone with a solid following, and someone who fits within your target market. If you're marketing to retired empty nesters, a 20-something influencer won't generate lots of sales, even if they have a huge following.

Don't worry if they don't have a giant following, of course – I've said it a thousand times already, but you're so much better targeting your exact market, versus casting a wide net.

Sometimes working with an influencer is as easy as swapping products for exposure. You send them x number of candles, they review it on their channel, and everyone is happy. Sometimes it's the influencer sharing your direct information or post, which isn't ideal – your influencer is their own person, with their own personality. People come for that, so trust them some to let that shine through.

Finding, and working, with the right influencers can really boost your brand for a very reasonable price. Don't hesitate to reach out via DM or website to any influencer you think hits the mark for your brand to discuss. The worst they can say is no – or give you an outlandish price to content ratio.

## What about Google Ads?

So we've got social media down pat. Let's talk for just a moment about a common way to advertise – Google Ads. First, I want to explain what they are and why I would/would not use them for your candle-making business.

First, let me educate you a bit on Google Ads. Purchasing ads on Google has been around forever, and businesses still use Google Ads for a reason. They really can work for your brand. With Google Ads, you can reach people who aren't on social media (i.e., they don't have a Facebook or Instagram page, but they do use the internet), or for those who only spend a small amount of time every day online.

These ads also offer a lot more features for you, the business, looking to advertise. Google doesn't necessarily target markets, but they target keywords. This means you're not going to be paying Google to only show your website to 20-something moms; you're going to be paying Google to show your website to everyone searching for your keyword of choice.

Some keywords that might apply? Organic candles, soy candles, hand-poured candles, natural candles, handmade candles. Think about the words that describe your business or your product, and how people would search to find you.

Google Ads is super easy to use, and really, you need very little knowledge of advertising or even the platform itself to start. If you jump in and you're immediately losing money, there are thousands of hours of free YouTube tutorials – but let's cover the basics, so you don't feel lost, and save you some time.

The most important thing is to ensure your landing page from the ad is relevant to your keyword and your business. If your customers are searching for hand-poured soy candles, don't take them to an About Us page – take them to the page where they can browse your candles.

Make sure that all the available ad content and all the relevant ad extensions are filled out and up to date. These little things are often overlooked but make a difference.

My final piece of advice comes to choosing keywords. Be thoughtful and careful in how you choose your Google Ads keywords, and think like your target market. What are they searching for? The more specific your keywords are, the more focused your results will be.

A keyword like "candles" is going to turn up approximately a zillion results (okay, not actually a zillion), but when you narrow that down to be more specific, people are more likely to click on it.

**To use, or not to use?**

This brings me to my last piece of advice: should you use Google Ads at all?

197

Generally, if you are making candles that most people can find locally or on a thousand different websites, Google Ads might not be for you—simply because most people don't do an online search when they buy candles. If they like homemade candles, they probably go to their local flea market or Whole Foods or Etsy shop. I believe very few people who want to buy candles will do a search online for candles.

However – and this is for someone out there, I'm sure of it – you may be the exception. Google Ads might be just what you need. Let me explain.

If you sell a rare, specialty type of candle – or one made with unique, in-demand ingredients – that is hard to find in stores or locally, Google Ads may be the best advertising for you to use.

For example, if you use all-natural, organic beeswax, then someone very well may search for that online. Or if you use therapeutic-grade essential oils to fragrance your candles, or pure coconut soap, or specific oils for meditation or relaxation or stress relief (you get the idea, very specialized) – then you may do great with Google Ads. Perhaps you might use a portion of your proceeds to benefit a certain nonprofit or cause, or use recyclable packaging. Just consider: who would do an online search for specialty candles, and what are they looking for? Be sure that you're using the right keywords to catch your target market, and Google Ads may work wonders for you.

## Free Alternatives to Ads

While these are the major forms of advertising that you're going to be using, there are other routes out there. These are some of the free advertisements you can do for your business that will generate interest and visitors.

**Blog posts** on your website about your process, your tools, or your life can generate interest. Share these on crafting sites, business boards, and more.

**Flyers** or brochures can go in local gathering places, coffee shops, and more. Print attractive flyers or business cards for yourself, and leave them places your target market hangs out. While this should never be your only way of advertisement, it's a great way to reach a new market that might not be spending as much time online.

**Be present:** Spend some time online where your target market also hangs out. Answer questions on Quora, find communities to promote and share your work on Reddit, and try to build a reputation of a brand people can trust and appreciate.

Don't hesitate to encourage your customers to leave good reviews about your products on social media platforms or other places online. This does nothing but improve your reputation, and gets your name out there.

## Should I Offer Discounts and Sales?

This is something only you can answer – but you know that everyone else does. If not sales, consider doing promotional items for holidays like Christmas, Halloween, Thanksgiving, Valentine's Day, Saint Patrick's Day, etc.

Gift sets for holidays are always a great seller, and if your customers know that you have a changing library of scents and products, then you're going to have more people come back again and again for new products.

If you have a lot of product and you need to move it quickly, or you want to boost sales, a sale week is totally fine! Be wary of relying on sales for all of your business, and make sure you're still making money on each item you sell. Even though you can sell more in quantity with a deep discount, you might not be able to make the same money.

## How Can I Get The Word Out?

It can be hard starting from scratch, so I'm going to encourage you for a moment to consider using your best resource available – friends and family. Think about the people you know that also fit into your target market  – or, at this point, at least near it.

Start a list of these people. Everyone who could be potential clients of yours, working from closest to you to farther out. Don't get hung up on specifics; just go for as many people as you can think of. We can always prune the list down later.

Do you have your list? Okay, scan it again, and think about how you can let these people know you're starting a candle business. Sure, you can send a Facebook message, shoot them a text, or even call them. And that would be fine, but you don't want to be seen as tacky, after all, and asking your close friends and family to buy something from you can come off that way.

A great marketing tool I recommend to all new businesses is **free samples**. Give out free samples to these people, with your labels clear and easy to read, and the location they can find your products at, whether it's your website or your Etsy page.

Send small, well-made, well-packaged candles home with friends and family with your business card, or a note about how you appreciate their support in your new business. Make sure they always know where they can purchase more from you, but don't pressure them into financially supporting you. It's a business, not a charity – let your high-quality product stand out.

## Listen to Feedback – All of It

Alright, once everyone on your list has gotten their samples, wait a week or two, and then do a gentle check-in. Ask for their feedback, their thoughts, their advice. Some people might not have burned their candles yet, and that's okay. People are busy, so please don't get mad when they can't prioritize your business over their lives.

It's hard to hear something negative about a product you feel strongly about, but it's important that you listen to what they have to say. If one person says they really didn't like the vanilla notes in your candle, well, maybe that scent isn't for them – but if five people tell you that it burnt bitter and left a lingering smell, they might be onto something.

You cannot let the people blindly praising your product or service inflate your ego to the point where you can't listen to constructive criticism. The only way you're going to get better and be successful is to respond to the negative and the positive feedback, even if you don't personally agree.

That said – not everyone is always right. Work to find a balance between solving real problems ("the tin heats up so quickly it left a mark on my wood table!") versus personal issues ("the rose notes gave me a headache").

Once you have heard everyone's feedback, take a look at your product again. Have you fixed any real issues? Do you have the best possible final product to sell? You're not looking for "perfect in every single way" – but then again, is "good enough" really, actually good enough? Ask yourself, would I pay for this product? If the answer is no, go back to the drawing board and start again.

Once you have a "yes, I would pay for this product," you're ready to really, truly get your business up and running, and move forward.

Are you excited? You should be!

# CHAPTER 13: WHERE SHOULD I SELL?

This is the million-dollar question: where should you sell your products? Great question! Every business is obviously going to have a different 'right' answer, and there are few 'wrong' answers in general, but let's go over your options. Should you sell online, locally, to friends and family, or all of the above? Let's look at some of these options.

## Things to Consider

If you're thinking about doing a portion, or even the bulk, of your sales in-person, there is a lot to think about. It's all going to come back to – you guessed it – your target market.

Where is your target marketing shopping and hanging out? Is it farmer's markets? Craft fairs? Weekend flea markets? Festivals? If your target demographic likes any of these places, you can set up stalls or tables to sell your goods. Make sure you present yourself in a professional, cohesive way – with your branding front and center, so people can identify with you immediately.

Don't limit yourself to just these options, though. A local hotel might be interested in candles or other scented products to put in their rooms, or in their lobby. Perhaps your favorite podcast (or a podcast your target audience listens to) has a shop. Reach out and see if they would be interested in custom-branded, custom blends for their customers – with your business name, of course.

Think outside the box: Are there little mom-and-pop shops or niche stores in your area that your target market shops at? Reach out and see if they would be interested in carrying your products, and helping you expand your brand.

What about events? Connecting with a major wedding venue and offering custom candles or custom labeling for weddings could be beneficial to you, the venue, and the newlywed couple. Realtors often make care packages for new homeowners, and high-end apartment complexes do the same. There are so many avenues you can go down to find prospective customers and expand your business.

Truly, the only limitation here is you. Where can you find your target market, and how can you reach them best?

## Online

First of all, I highly encourage selling **online**. You can set up your website to directly take orders, and this will help you cut out the middle man and reduce any fees you might encounter. Because yes, most online storefronts that offer to sell your products for you will take a cut.

Other than your website and online storefront, what are some other options?

**Etsy** is a huge crafting utopia that has changed and evolved a lot over the past few years. Some estimate it has quadrupled in sales during the 2020 pandemic. More and more, drop shippers and bulk buyers are filling Etsy pages with questionable merchandise. This doesn't mean you shouldn't use Etsy, though – because this is often the first platform people go to for buying unique, handmade products just like yours!

Make sure you understand all the fees associated with Etsy, and what you're going to be spending upfront. There is a fee for every single item you list on Etsy, whether it sells or not, and every 4 months you need to renew that listing and pay the fee.

There is also a transaction fee associated with Etsy, which is 5% right now. For every $100 in candles you sell on the platform, Etsy will take $5. Depending on how many candles you're selling, this can add up fast, but it isn't the end of the world.

For many starting businesses, Etsy provides an amazing platform to get their brand and their products out there. It's also a trusted retail store, and customers won't' hesitate to use their credit card information for purchases.

Overall, despite the fees, I recommend Etsy as a selling platform – especially at first.

## Facebook

**Facebook Marketplace** is somewhere I see a lot of new businesses trying to get their feet wet.

The marketplace can be really excellent if you live in an area that is busy or has many people using it, but I would caution you to be careful. Not only are you meeting strangers (do I sound like my mother?), but you have no promise they will also meet you. You could easily get stood up, or put yourself in a bad position. There is an option in Marketplace to ship the product, and generally if you use a site like PayPal to process the funding, this is probably a safe option.

On the plus side, it doesn't cost anything to post Facebook Marketplace listings of your candles, and you can build a loyal local customer base. This is exceptionally good if and when you go into local stores to ask about them carrying your product – you can easily say you've sold 300 candles in a year to everyone in your zip code.

Overall, I would advise caution using Facebook Marketplace, but you don't have to avoid it entirely.

**Facebook Groups** are another great resource, just like Marketplace. Find local crafting supply groups or groups that promote local businesses, and post about your own business there. You can offer 'local discounts' or 'local packages' if you want, and it's a good way to get your name out there and get a lot of viewers.

Once again, use caution with local Facebook groups, just like with the Marketplace. But I would still use Facebook Groups, especially if your target market is near you physically and uses these same platforms.

## Local Shops & Markets

Don't forget brick-and-mortar shops in your area! You can also approach local gift shops, boutiques, and consignment stores that may specialize in locally made items.

Even some Whole Foods grocery stores have a section of locally made products like soaps, lotions, and candles. Before you submit a proposal, do some research into what they are already offering and the price points of the products. Make sure you understand what the shop will offer you for each sale; some take a percentage on consignments while others will simply buy your candles for an agreed-upon price and resell them at a higher price. It's best to be clear on the details ahead of time.

Consider farmer's markets, local flea markets, and other pop-up events as a chance to sell your goods. Be sure you bring plenty of inventory and that you have your sales face on – as in, you're feeling as polite and happy as possible, and ready to answer the same 3 or 4 questions over and over again.

These are also great networking opportunities. You can meet the owners of local shops that might like to sell your goods, connect with creators that do similar work (maybe they'll want to collaborate at some point) and find out about other events you've never heard of.

Often for farmer's markets, you need to register early and make a commitment for a set number of hours. You're paying for your spot whether you use it or not, basically. With a flea market or other craft market, it's a little more flexible – you can buy a table for a weekend, a month, or several months.

If you're planning on selling in person, make sure you have a table that makes your goods look nice. A quality tablecloth, attractive shelves or positioning, and a variety of goods are all important. You can easily make shelving for yourself, or ask a friend who likes woodworking. I've also had great luck finding unique pieces at thrift stores or flea markets that you can paint and reuse.

A **business card** should go in every bag or with every purchase, and everyone who walks up to your stall should immediately know who you are and what you're about. That's part of a good brand, but also just part of doing good business.

If you're not a 'people person' and you don't like meeting lots of folks, talking to them about your candles, or answering lots of questions, I don't recommend selling in-person like this. You know yourself, so be honest here. You could also easily hire a friend or family member to come with you and handle the bulk of the interactions for the day, if that makes financial sense.

Another way to get the word out about your business locally is to offer free products for special community events (at churches, fundraisers, etc) in exchange for a mention of your business. Remember, I got my start by supplying candles for my friend's wedding.

# Chapter 14: The Legal Side of Things

Stop! Before you pour a candle! Before you hire a graphic designer, or make your first Facebook post! It's time to talk about everyone's least favorite part: legalities.

There are a lot of technical things that go along with this. None of them are fun, all of them involve paperwork, and yes, you absolutely must do these in order to have a business.

I don't know what state you're living in, or what country, so I can't give you specific advice. But what I can do is go over the most important things you need, like registering your business, paying taxes, handling your accounts, and keeping all your finances in order.

This is the least fun and arguably the most important part of owning your own business.

If at any point you feel overwhelmed with the process, or your sales have exploded and you can't keep up, you absolutely can and should hire someone else to help out. But we're not there yet, so let's dive into it together.

## Defining Yourself as a Business

The first thing you need to consider is when/if to register your business as a business. Many businesses such as ours start out small, making their products from home, learning as you go, with yourself as the only employee. Then, once the business starts making a profit (making more money than you are expending), it may be time to register with local and federal agencies.

For instance, you may not realize that the IRS could consider you merely a hobby rather than a business if you are not making a profit for three out of five consecutive years. ***This is an important distinction, as a hobby cannot deduct any expenses or losses on your tax return.***

So, once you've gotten your business off the ground and are making more than you spend, it may be time to claim your status as a business.

**Research your state:** The first legal step you need to take is to make your business official by registering it with your state. Each state has different rules and regulations, so you're going to want to dive deep into your state's official website to figure out exactly what permits and registrations you need. Some states do not require a single-person business operating under the owner's name to register at all. (But remember, if you don't register your business, you could miss out on personal liability protection, legal benefits, and tax benefits.)

So it's best to check with your state and local governments. Generally, you need fewer permits for candles than, say, if you were making food products, but there will be regulations for you to follow.

**Double-checking your name:** While you're poking around, take a moment and check your state's business records. They should be on file and relatively easy to search through. Make sure that no one else has the name of your company already registered. While this could be crushing, it definitely should be one of the early steps in your process.

Having a few backup names for your brand is always a good idea.

Also check both federal and state trademark records. In the U.S., federal trademarks are handled by the U.S. Patent and Trademark Office (uspto.gov) whereas state trademarks are handled by the secretary of state office for each state. You want to know: Does anyone have your name trademarked? Does anyone have an extremely similar name trademarked? Also, you'll want to check on social media platforms, do an extensive Google search, and check domain name availability. This is so important!

Okay, so you've got a name, and you know no one else is running a business under it. What's next?

## Business Registration and Types

There are several ways to register your business name in order to protect it (Entity name, Trademark, DBAs, and Domain names). There are also several different types of businesses, ranging from sole proprietorship, partnerships, LLCs, and various types of corporations. Let's take a look at three common types of small businesses:

| Sole Proprietorship | Partnership | LLC |
|---|---|---|
| • Owned and operated by one person. | • Owned and operated by 2+ people. Each contributes money, property, labor or skill; shares profits &losses. | • A hybrid business entity that combines aspects of a coproration and partnership. |
| • **Advantages:** Easy to start, owner makes all decisions, keeps all profits, is his/her own boss. | • **Advantages**: Easy to start, more ways to raise capital, shared skills and decisions. | • **Advantages:** Offers limited liability protection, tax deductions and flexibility. |
| • **Disadvantages:** Owner liable for all debts and assets, must work long hours. Difficult to raise capital to start. All risk falls on owner. | • **Disadvantages**: Each partner is liable for debts, can make decisions, share profits. Conflict possible. | • **Disadvantages:** Profits may be subject to self-employment taxes. |

To learn more about these and types of corporations, visit www.sba.gov for a guide to differentiating between the small business types. You'll also find out how to register your business, get federal and state tax ID numbers, apply for licenses and permits, open a business bank account, and get business insurance.

But don't worry about all of these things at first. If you're just starting out, chances are you can keep it simple.

Most candle-makers start out as a **sole proprietorship**. This means that you are the sole employee and owner of the company. By choosing sole-proprietorship, you're saying, Hey, this business is my own, no one else's. I'm the owner; I do it all. No one can hold any other shares in your business. You also don't have to file separate returns for the business, which is nice.

When filing taxes, usually a sole proprietor will use your own Social Security number (though you can register for a special tax ID if you like). It's a simple business structure, but it will not cover you in the case of an accident and doesn't afford many tax advantages. So if you take on more risk—such as hiring other employees or opening up a brick-and-mortar shop—you'll want to become an LLC.

If you're ready to expand, you may want to register as an **LLC**, or a Limited Liability Company. You might be thinking, "Why would I spend more money to do an LLC when it's cheaper and makes sense to do a sole-proprietorship?" That's a fair question. Perhaps the biggest reason is that being an LLC protects you as a person from any legal repercussions.

Let's say that someone improperly uses your candles, and they burn down their home. Yikes, that's awful. To get even, they come after your company. That's really awful. In a situation of sole-proprietorship, the courts would come after not just the business, but you. Anything you own could be considered an asset, and fair game for seizure.

With an LLC, only the company's assets (not yours) would be at risk, and the company would be liable to deal with any legal issues. LLCs are a little more complicated to set up, and cost a bit more, but they are by far worth the investment. It protects you as a person, and is better in the long run for when your business grows and you may want to bring on investors. Again, do some research on sba.gov to learn about the benefits of LLCs.

In my opinion? I *highly recommend* you going with an LLC. It protects everyone involved.

## So How Do I Start An LLC?

If you decide to register as an LLC, I can offer you a few tips to get started on the right track.

Head to your state's Secretary of State website, or go into the office. You need to get an LLC Articles of Organization from there. Fill out that form.

Some states need you to publish a notice in the local newspaper stating your intention to form an LLC. It reminds me of an old-timey business situation, but you should be able to find the information from the Secretary of State's office. If they do not require it, don't bother – it's just a waste of money!

Submit your completed form to the Secretary of State's office, along with the fee associated. It can range from $150 to $900 depending on what state you are in, so make sure you do your research and calculate this into your startup costs as appropriate.

In some states, you'll be asked to pay a corporate tax as soon as you file. This is a bummer, but if your state requires it, what can you do?

**Taxes: Everyone's Favorite Thing**

My father used to tell me there were only two certainties in the world: taxes and death. He wasn't wrong, and taxes are very important in your business. This is honestly where a lot of new businesses fall apart, because they're so intimidated by the taxes and fees associated. It doesn't have to be scary – I promise.

You need an EIN number, or an Employer Identification Number. This is pretty easy to get, so don't stress.

Head to the IRS website, and find your state's official site through there. Fill out the requested information on your state's site, but do not close the page. It won't save.

Once everything is filled out, you'll be directed back to the IRS's site, where you'll need to provide yet more information. These are all pretty easy, and questions you should have answers to.

Once you have everything filled out on the IRS's site, you will obtain the EIN assigned to you. Save the number, and you can close the site.

Then, go back to your state's application, and input your EIN.

Piece of cake.

Once you've got all those annoying-but-easy steps finished, you need to go to the state's taxing authority, or the revenue department, to pay any state income taxes to get yourself started. You will also probably need to apply for a tax seller's permit with your state, which should go through the Department of Revenue.

Alright, taxes are complete. Congratulations!

## The Little Things to Take Care Of

It's very important that you're set up with both the state and the local government. Each county might handle local businesses differently, and you need to make sure to get on top of that before you start, you know, running your business.

Check your county for any local-level permits or registrations you need, including zoning laws, health permits, or fire inspections. These seem like a hassle, and you might even think you can skate past doing some of this, but it's always worth it to keep everything above board at the start.

Most of the time, the biggest permits and inspection needs come from companies that make food-grade products. You're not making chocolate or baked goods, so that's already a win for your direction.

## Banking & Accounting

You've got a business, and an LLC, and all your permits are in place. It's now time to get your finances in order.

I recommend you use a dedicated business banking account and a business line of credit. You can use the same bank you use for your personal banking, or you can shop around and find who has the best rates and benefits for small businesses, but make sure you keep your personal assets separate from your business assets. (Again, you can check out the article on sba.gov about opening a business bank account.)

Opening a dedicated business bank account is good business practice even if you set up a sole-proprietorship and not an LLC. Don't mix your own money with business money, or your accounting is going to be a serious headache.

Speaking of headaches – accounting sounds very intimidating, but it's not so bad. The number one most important thing you should remember if you take away nothing else from this chapter is to keep accurate and detailed records, of everything. Seriously, every expense in or out. Use envelopes to organize what you spend on equipment, supplies, advertising, etc. Then keep detailed records of your sales and revenue.

This is going to make filing your taxes a whole lot easier come the beginning of the year, and it also is just good business practice. You should be able to look back and see immediately how much you've spent, how much you've invested, and what you're bringing in.

Most small businesses use QuickBooks, which starts at about $12 a month. If you're very intimidated, you can hire a part-time bookkeeper for a few hours a week or a month to handle it (ranging from about $20 - $50 per hour). But it's going to save you money to do it yourself, especially at first.

## Do I Need a Business Line of Credit?

This is a question only you, with knowledge of your finances and your credit history, can answer. If you can float your startup costs, you may not need to take out a business line of credit or deal with business credit cards. If you need a little financial boost to afford everything, this might be an option.

In general, a business credit card is a better idea than a loan, especially if your expenses are relatively low. Most business credit cards have zero percent APR for a set time and bonuses, like miles or rewards, that add up and can help your business grow.

Think long and hard before you take out money for your business, and don't get blinded by a bank offering you a high line of credit or a big loan number. You'll have to pay all of it back eventually, so only take out or spend what you can manage.

A business credit card or a line of credit can be the difference between success and failure. That extra money and cushion can really come in handy, and help you get your business off the ground. Just make sure you use the money responsibly, and don't get carried away with it.

## Yes, There Are Business Taxes

And yes, you need to pay them. Again, each state will handle these a little differently, but we can do an overview to get you prepared.

You'll need to pay income tax on the profit of the company. For many businesses, especially small ones like yours starting out, income tax is passed onto the owner's personal tax returns.

You're going to need to complete a Schedule C as part of your personal tax return when you go to file. A Schedule C is going to help you determine the net income of your company, so you can pay the appropriate taxes.

*Pro Tip:* Before you file, look into the Qualified Business Income Deduction. Not every small business will qualify, but if you do, you can get up to 20% off of qualified income until the year 2025. This can be a big help for small businesses concerned about their taxes.

## What Is Self-Employment Tax?

Bad news: you're also going to need to pay self-employment taxes. Even if you are your own only employee, you need to pay these taxes. These basically pay into Medicare and Social Security, and they are based on the net income of the business, nothing else.

You need to make sure you're paying estimated taxes each quarter. Essentially, you're telling the IRS how much money you've made and paying your estimated owed taxes ahead of time. Normally, they're usually due in the middle of the month after that quarter.

So, for the dates September 1 through December 31, they will be due sometime in the middle of January. Each day the specific date shifts by one or two days, depending on when a weekend falls – if January 15th is a Saturday, it will move to that next

Monday. If the 15th is, say, a Wednesday, they will be due that Wednesday.

If you do not pay each quarter, you will be charged a *penalty*. This isn't just to make tax time easier come April; it is required by the IRS.

Finally, let's talk about gross receipt tax and state income tax. The majority of states have a state income tax for businesses, but some – like Texas or Nevada – impose what is called a gross receipt tax. This is essentially just a tax on your revenue that is either in addition, or instead of, your state income tax.

In some states, a sole-proprietor will not have to pay this tax. Make sure you look closely at each state's requirements. I know, this all sounds so complicated – but it's really only tough the first time. It does get a lot easier. By your second year, you'll feel like a pro.

## What Counts as a Tax Deduction?

Some more good news (especially for LLCs): a lot of your expenses will count as **tax deductions**. It might seem like a small amount at first, but it really does add up, and at the end of the year you're going to be happy you kept track of all of this.

Save all of your business-related receipts. Business meals, or working lunches, are considered business expenses and are tax-deductible. So are home office expenses, like printers, desks, computer equipment, paper, even ink, and toner. Your phone and internet expenses? If you use that for your business, they are also considered business expenses and tax-deductible. Again, make sure you keep all of these receipts in a dedicated space where you can find them easily.

## So, How Do You Take Payments?

Alright! We're getting into fun things again. Let's talk about how you can accept payment for your goods. There are a few different options for you.

Your bank account is your number one option, obviously. Many banks offer small businesses the ability to accept payment. You'll need a merchant account if you want to want to take credit card payments, but that is something you can discuss with your business bank. Each bank will obviously handle things a little differently, so make sure you do your research on what banks are available in your area and what they offer. I could recommend a number of good business banks, but if none are within 30 miles from you, it does you no good.

I do recommend choosing a credit union if you can. Generally, they have the best rates, the best policies, and the best customer service. If you can find a local credit union that handles business accounts, you'll be in good hands.

PayPal is a super common, super secure way to do business. The majority of small businesses online have PayPal as an option, with some exclusively taking PayPal. It's important to know that PayPal isn't a free service, though – they shave between 0.7% and 2.9% off of every transaction, plus an extra 30 cents on top of that. The exact numbers will depend on your sales volume.

However, all you have to do is add the "Buy Now" button to your website, and PayPal does the rest. Is this ease of use and security worth the tradeoff? For many, it is.

Other popular choices include Stripe (which allows both local currencies and Bitcoin, recurring billing, and fraud protection), Pay with Amazon, and Square.

All of these choices are going to take some sort of cut from your profits; it's just a fact of life. Make sure you go with a reputable company that you trust, and that your customers will trust. If your customers think your online payment method seems shady, they're not going to submit their credit card information. Can you blame them?

*Pro tip:* Lots of small businesses have seen great success with Shopify, a relatively new platform. Shopify basically handles everything, and it can help you set up your website, create a domain, keep track of orders and inventory, and a whole lot more. They have a buy button, they can handle credit cards; it can be a one-stop-shop. If you're struggling with what choice to make, be sure to check it out. Shopify is being used on thousands of smaller websites and businesses, and making it easier than ever for businesses just like us to have a functioning website that takes payment.

I'm not affiliated with Shopify in any way, but I know many happy clients, so it's worth checking out!

# CHAPTER 15: KEEP PUSHING, YOU GOT THIS!

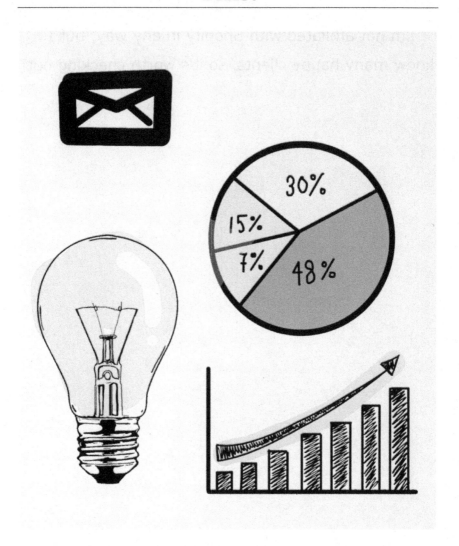

It's easy to get discouraged as you move forward when you don't feel like you're hitting your goals fast enough. Not enough sales, not enough leads, just not enough. I understand. You've put so much time and effort into your business, and all you're asking for is some payoff, right?

Think about running your business like raising a child. It takes years for your child to learn to crawl, to walk, to run, to speak, to sing, to read, to write, to do basic math. Time is the secret ingredient. It's not going to happen overnight, and learning to accept that is a big part of running a business. Give it some time.

## Your Business Requires Attention

Let's stick with the child analogy for a moment. If your business is like a child, it's going to need attention, love, and stimulation. You can't just toss it out in the world and hope for the best – you're going to need to really pay attention and **guide** the business to success every step of the way.

If you're feeling overwhelmed with a certain aspect of the business, you can always **outsource** some of it. If accounting seems overwhelming and you find yourself ignoring your books instead of doing them regularly, hiring someone part-time might be worth the money. If social media overwhelms you and you dread opening Instagram or Facebook, hiring someone to manage your SM accounts could be more than worth the investment.

*Just stay on top of it*. This constant attention is important, and as you continue to grow, you'll absolutely need to outsource some aspects to scale up. One person alone can't run a huge, successful candle-making business, after all!

Attention should also be paid to your business as it *changes and grows*. Keep an eye on prices and profit margins, on customer feedback, on your suppliers. Yes, some of this is in the business plan – but as you grow, you're going to evolve, too, and that is very important. A successful business can adapt and change to meet its needs.

*Celebrate your successes*, and make sure your goals are broken up into easy-to-meet segments that will keep you motivated. If you're hitting goals and moving forward, you're going to want to pay attention to your business and keep coming back for more.

## Don't Be Afraid to Add/Change/Update

A lot of small business owners are nervous about changing or adding to their business, because they don't want to alienate their current customers. But this isn't the best mentality for success. Growth is good! Don't be afraid to offer new product lines, new scents, or new types of candles.

People love new things, and if you're known as a store that regularly updates and changes their inventory, or brings in new seasonal products, you're giving your customers a reason to come back and buy more. If your stock is always the same, they will only return once they have finished that candle and need another one. But if you have seasonal lines or new products, they will buy again even if they're not done with their current products.

You can also branch out and offer new types of products, like home fragrances, wax melts, lamps, and more. Soaps, skincare, or other products might complement your current line. What else does your target market like? What are they buying, and can you provide it to them, too? Don't add junk to your site just to sell more, of course, but if you can offer a quality product that matches your market, it's a great opportunity.

## Improve, Adapt, Overcome

It's a proven fact that companies that adapt quickly and are willing to change direction to meet the market's needs do better. The faster and better you can make these changes, the better your business will do.

Pay attention to your target market, and what they like. What trends are happening that you can capitalize on? (For example, eco-friendly products, or new scents that are becoming popular.) The faster you can move and offer them, the better you'll do. And once you're known as someone that can, you're going to have people coming back again and again.

Don't be afraid to send out surveys to customers. What did they like? What didn't they like? Getting your customer's feedback will allow you to keep changing and adapting in a way that's meaningful to your target market. It's hard to listen to something negative about your business, but it truly is the only way you're able to keep growing and changing. Not listening to the negatives is so dangerous, and is a sure-fire way to stall your progress.

If you find yourself struggling or getting discouraged, I encourage you to read through this book again. Do you need to take another look at your marketing? Your packaging? Your logo design? Your candles themselves, or the quality-to-price you're putting out?

If you're giving your business the love and attention it deserves, and you're not making any sales, there's something up. Don't be afraid to hire a consultant or an expert in this business to help you figure out where you're going wrong. It might feel like you're giving up by reaching out for help, but these people exist for a reason. Getting an outside opinion can be incredibly important and helpful.

## It's OK to Admit You Don't Know Something

Going into business for yourself can be crazy intimidating, and there are likely going to be times that you feel overwhelmed or unsure. There are points where you're going to want to give up, or you're going to be staring at something for a long time and admit, *Wow, I really don't know how to do this/what I'm doing/where to start.*

That's all okay!

**Don't give up.** We all have been there. Even people who graduated school with business degrees have had moments of uncertainty; and for us, people trying their best with what they've got? We're going to get overwhelmed and frustrated.

## Keep learning

I encourage you not only to take full advantage of this book, but to use the school of Google and YouTube wisely. You're not the first person to ever make their own candles, or go into business making candles, and that is a great thing. It means you can **learn from others'** experiences and mistakes, and end up with a better finished product, faster.

Do all of the research you can, all the time. Ask questions, talk to friends and other vendors and ask for advice. Absorb wisdom from blog posts and other creators. Go on forums and ask specific questions about specific problems and to get advice. The internet is an incredible place, and 20 years ago this would have been unthinkable – and so much harder.

You don't have to struggle. Be willing to learn, to put your concern to the side, and you can make this a great business.

## Go, Make Candles, and Be Successful!

It's time for you to take the leap. Do you feel prepared? This book will always be here for you if you have questions or concerns. Feel free to bookmark sections, to re-read something again, or revisit when you're having a hard time.

Your business can be successful. You've got this! If you made it this far, you have the interest and the drive. I won't lie to you and say it won't be hard work and a lot of effort, but a successful business is worth every drop of sweat or frustrated tear.

As I said at first: *Congratulations* on making this major step and deciding to start your own business. Now, you have the knowledge to make it a reality. Go for your dream!

If you have found anything in this book helpful to you, I would love to hear back from you through an online review of my book. All the best to you in your new business venture!

Made in the USA
Las Vegas, NV
27 November 2024

12788013R00134